World's Greatest BIBLE Puzzles

Volume 2
SUDOKU

BARBOUR
PUBLISHING

Print ISBN 978-1-61626-920-3

Published by Barbour Publishing, Inc., P.O. Box 719, Uhrichsville, Ohio 44683, www.barbourbooks.com

Our mission is to publish and distribute inspirational products offering exceptional value and biblical encouragement to the masses.

ecpa Member of the Evangelical Christian Publishers Association

Printed in the United States of America.

WELCOME TO WORLD'S GREATEST BIBLE PUZZLES, VOLUME 2—SUDOKU!

Millions worldwide have discovered the joy of sudoku—the puzzle that tests your skills of logic. The rapid growth in sudoku's popularity has rightly been called a phenomenon.

But what in the world is "Bible sudoku"? We're glad you asked!

World's Greatest Bible Puzzles, Volume 2—Sudoku combines the enjoyment of solving a sudoku puzzle with the challenge of Bible trivia. First, you put your scripture knowledge to the test, answering scripture-based questions to determine either the numerical or letter-based "givens" for each puzzle. Then you prove your logic abilities by completing the sudoku grid.

Here's how it works exactly:

Number-based puzzles

1. Each puzzle begins with a blank 9 x 9 grid. A coordinate system—with the letters A through I across the top, and the numbers 1 through 9 down the left side—will help you place the "givens," or starter numbers, generated by the Bible trivia questions.
2. For each puzzle, trivia questions will be answered by the numbers 1 through 9. The coordinates with each question (for example, A1, C9, H3) indicate where you should insert that particular answer into the sudoku grid. If you don't know the answer and want to find out from the Bible, references are provided. Or if you're really eager to get started, the answers are shown, upside down, underneath the puzzle grid.
3. Once you've inserted the givens into the grid, you can solve the sudoku puzzle. The goal of sudoku is to place the numbers 1 through 9 in each row, each column, and each of nine 3 x 3 mini-grids (the white and shaded

areas) within the larger puzzle. Numbers can never be duplicated in a row, column, or 3 x 3 grid—so use you skills of deduction to determine what numbers can or can't go into a particular box.

Letter-based puzzles

1. Each 9 x 9 grid includes "givens," as with traditional sudoku puzzles. But in this case, the givens are letters. The nine letters in each row, column, and 3 x 3 mini-grid will spell out a biblical word or phrase. Each word or phrase is taken directly from the King James Version of the Bible, unless a "/" is seen, in which case a modern equivalent is used in the puzzle. For example, "to keep/_____ the way" indicates that the KJV term "keep" will be replaced by another word; the context of the puzzle should help you determine the correct usage.
2. Each puzzle has a hint with a reference beneath it.
3. Letter-based puzzles are solved in the same manner as the number-based sudoku. Instead of using nine different numbers, you will use nine different letters. When solving, make sure that no letter repeats within any row, within any column, or within any of the nine 3 x 3 mini-grids.

Special thanks to our puzzle designers, Sara Stoker, Carrie Brown, Ellen Caughey, N. Teri Grottke, and Conover Swofford.

We hope you enjoy *World's Greatest Bible Puzzles, Volume 2—Sudoku!*

PUZZLE 1

	A	B	C	D	E	F	G	H	I
1		H				T	M	O	
2	A	T					S		
3	O		L	M				H	I
4				T	I	E			
5	E			A		O			H
6	T			S	H	M			L
7			T					I	
8		L	A					M	
9	S		O	E		L	H	A	T

Hint: Row 6

Esau went __ ________ to get himself yet another wife. (Genesis 28:9)

PUZZLE 2

For B2, I3, D6, G7, A9
How many pieces were some of the Lord's prophets sawed into? (Hebrews 11:37)

For C1, H3, F4, A5, B7, I8
How many vials in Revelation contained plagues? (Revelation 21:9)

For C2, E5, F7
How many hundred men came with Esau to meet Jacob? (Genesis 32:6)

For D7, H9
How many sons were born to King David in Jerusalem? (1 Chronicles 3:5–8)

For E1, I7, A8, F9
How many evil spirits, looking like frogs, did John see coming from a dragon's mouth? (Revelation 16:13)

For E3, G4, D5, F8, I2
How many hundred years did Shem live after he had Arphaxad? (Genesis 11:11)

For F2, C3, B5
How many years was Abdon judge of Israel? (Judges 12:13–14)

For G1, A3, B4, H5
How many Hebrews did Moses see an Egyptian beating up? (Exodus 2:11)

For H1, D3, I4, B6, G8, C7
In John's vision of heaven, how many wings did each of the four beasts have? (Revelation 4:8)

	A	B	C	D	E	F	G	H	I
1									
2									
3									
4									
5									
6									
7									
8									
9									

Starter Numbers in Order:
2, 7, 4, 9, 3, 5, 8, 1, 6

PUZZLE 3

For B6, C7, G8, I3
How many golden lampstands are mentioned in Revelation 1:20?

For A6, C8, D3, E7, F4, G1, I9
How many young men refused the king's meat? (Daniel 1:11–12)

For A4, D6, G5, H2
How many verses are in Psalm 100?

For D5, E9, F3, G6, I1
How many coins did the good Samaritan give the innkeeper? (Luke 10:35)

For A9, B5, C3, E6
In the ten plagues visited on Egypt, what number plague was locusts? (Exodus 7:14–10:4)

For A7, C2, G3, H6
How many friends initially came to comfort Job? (Job 2:11)

For A5, B8, D2, E4, F7, H3
How many fingers on each hand did the man of stature in 2 Samuel 21:20 have?

For B3, F6, G2, H9
How many sheep did the shepherd lose in Matthew 18:10–14?

For A3, C6, D4, F2
How many sons did Shem and Aram have? (1 Chronicles 1:17)

	A	B	C	D	E	F	G	H	I
1									
2									
3									
4									
5									
6									
7									
8									
9									

Starter Numbers in Order:
7, 4, 5, 2, 8, 3, 6, 1, 9

PUZZLE 4

For A6, B9, C3, E2, F4, G5
How many sons did Perez have? (1 Chronicles 2:5)

For C1
On which day of creation did God call the gathered waters "Seas"? (Genesis 1:10–13)

For A9, I3
According to Proverbs, how many things can the earth not bear? (Proverbs 30:21)

For A7, B3, C4, E9, F5, H8, I2
In the city called "The LORD is there," how many gates were named for Gad? (Ezekiel 48:34–35)

For E7, G9, H6, I1
How many sons did Leah have? (Genesis 30:20)

For A1, C7, D8, F3
How many years was Aeneas in bed with palsy? (Acts 9:33)

For B7, C5, D6, G8, H3, I4
How many hundred years did Shem live after he had Arphaxad? (Genesis 11:11)

For B6, F1, H5
How many sons did Abihail have? (1 Chronicles 5:13–14)

For E8, I5
How many cubits long was Og's bed? (Deuteronomy 3:11)

	A	B	C	D	E	F	G	H	I
1									
2									
3									
4									
5									
6									
7									
8									
9									

Starter Numbers in Order:
2, 3, 4, 1, 6, 8, 5, 7, 9

PUZZLE 5

For B1, C5, G4
How many generations did Job live to see? (Job 42:16)

For A3, D7, E4
When Israel's enemies come up against them, in how many ways will they flee? (Deuteronomy 28:7)

For A2, E6, F1, I7
". . .than of the ninety and _____ which went not astray." (Matthew 18:13)

For A7, C3, D8, H1
How many years old was the she-goat used in Abraham's covenant with God? (Genesis 15:9)

For B2, D1, F6, I4
How many hundred men followed David before he was king? (1 Samuel 23:13)

For D2, E8, G7, H6, I1
How many hundred years did Adam live after he had Seth? (Genesis 5:4)

For A9, D3, E5, H8, I2
How many tables were to be placed on the right side of the temple? (2 Chronicles 4:8)

For D4, E1
How many years did Elah reign in Israel? (1 Kings 16:8)

For B8, D5, H7
In the city called "The Lord is there," how many gates were named for Asher? (Ezekiel 48:34)

	A	B	C	D	E	F	G	H	I
1									
2									
3									
4									
5									
6									
7									
8									
9									

Starter Numbers in Order:
4, 7, 9, 3, 6, 8, 5, 2, 1

PUZZLE 6

For A5, C1, E8, F3, G6, H2, I7
How many years did Paul stay in his own rented house in Rome? (Acts 28:30)

For A9, C2, D7, G8, H3, I4
How many measures of barley will sell for a penny during the tribulation? (Revelation 6:6)

For B3, D5, E2, I6
How many of the tabernacle curtains were to be coupled together? (Exodus 26:3)

For A3, B4, C8, E9, F2
What was the approximate height in feet of Goliath? (1 Samuel 17:4)

For B8, D2, G7, I3
How many days after Jesus said, "There be some of them that stand here, which shall not taste of death, till they have seen the kingdom of God come with power," did Peter, James, and John see Jesus transfigured on a mountain? (Mark 9:1–2)

For C3, F6, G4, H9
On what day were male babies—descendants of Abraham—to be circumcised? (Genesis 17:12)

For A8, B1, D3, F5, H4, I9
How many heads does the beast of Revelation have? (Revelation 17:7)

For B7, D9, F4
According to Joseph's plan, after paying Egypt's tax, how many fifths of the harvest were left for the people? (Genesis 47:24)

For B2, C9, F7, G3
How many tenths of an ephah is an omer? (Exodus 16:36)

	A	B	C	D	E	F	G	H	I
1									
2									
3									
4									
5									
6									
7									
8									
9									

Starter Numbers in Order:
2, 3, 5, 9, 6, 8, 7, 4, 1

PUZZLE 7

For C3, D1, G9, I4
How were the disciples sent out? (Mark 6:7)

For B5, C7, F1, G4, I3
How many hundred did Adino slay at one time? (2 Samuel 23:8)

For A4, C1, D5, F7
How many days per week was Israel allowed to work? (Exodus 20:9)

For C2, D7, E4, F3, H5, I9
How many thousand proverbs did Solomon speak? (1 Kings 4:32)

For A7, B1, C4, E5
In the list of the Ten Commandments, what number commandment says, "Thou shalt not commit adultery?" (Exodus 20:14)

For A1, F5, G7, I2
Besides the first four, how many other sons did David have with Bathsheba? (1 Chronicles 3:8)

For B3, E7, H6
How many dressed sheep did Abigail take to David? (1 Samuel 25:18)

For A6, C9, D8, E1, G3, H7, I5
In a vision of Daniel, how many heads were on the beast like a leopard? (Daniel 7:6)

For C8, E9, F6, H1
How many kings of Aphek did Joshua smite? (Joshua 12:7, 18)

	A	B	C	D	E	F	G	H	I
1									
2									
3									
4									
5									
6									
7									
8									
9									

Starter Numbers in Order:
2, 8, 6, 3, 7, 9, 5, 4, 1

PUZZLE 8

For B6, C7
How many daughters did Reuel have? (Exodus 2:16)

For B5, C3, E6
What chapter of Romans contains in verse 28 the assurance that God works everything together for our good?

For A6, D3, F4, G1, I9
How many sons did Ham have? (1 Chronicles 1:8)

For A4, G5, H2
Which of the first nine chapters of Acts deals with Ananias and Sapphira?

For B3, F6, G2, H9
How many coins were lost in Luke 15:8–10?

For A7, C2, G3
How many months was Jehoiachin king of Judah? (2 Kings 24:8)

For A5, B8, D2, E4, F7, H3
In the list of the sons of Jesse in 1 Chronicles 2:13–15, what number son is Ozem?

For D5, E9, F3, G6, I1
How many sons did Naomi have? (Ruth 1:2)

For C6, D4, F2
How many beatitudes are listed in Matthew 5:3–11?

	A	B	C	D	E	F	G	H	I
1									
2									
3									
4									
5									
6									
7									
8									
9									

Starter Numbers in Order:
7, 8, 4, 5, 1, 3, 6, 2, 9

PUZZLE 9

For C4, F5, G1
How many sons of Anak did Caleb defeat? (Joshua 15:14)

For A8, B4, D5, F9, G6, H7
In David's confrontation with Nabal, how many hundred "abode by the stuff"? (1 Samuel 25:13)

For C5, D7, E3, F6, G4, H9
According to Eliphaz, how many troubles would God deliver Job from? (Job 5:19)

For B7, E5, F2, H1
How many chamberlains did King Ahasuerus have? (Esther 1:10)

For D6, E9, F1, G3
How many principal men were raised up? (Micah 5:5)

For A6, B1, E7, G8, H2, I5
"Be baptized every ___ of you in the name of Jesus Christ for the remission of sins." (Acts 2:38)

For A9, D1, E4, F8, G7, H5
How many hundred thousand fighting men were numbered in Judah? (2 Samuel 24:9)

For A4, D2, I8
". . .three thousand ___ hundred and thirty." (Nehemiah 7:38)

For C7, G2, H8, I6
How many thousand stalls did Solomon have? (2 Chronicles 9:25)

	A	B	C	D	E	F	G	H	I
1									
2									
3									
4									
5									
6									
7									
8									
9									

Starter Numbers in Order:
3, 2, 9, 7, 8, 1, 5, 6, 4

PUZZLE 10

	A	B	C	D	E	F	G	H	I
1	H		I		O		E		
2		M			E		Y	K	
3		Y	N		K		I		O
4				M					
5			O		N	H		L	
6	M	E			L	O	K		N
7	Y						L		M
8	N	L			I				K
9		H	K		M	Y		O	E

Hint: Column F

God promised the Hebrew slaves a land flowing with _____ and _____. (Exodus 3:8)

	A	B	C	D	E	F	G	H	I
1	G		S			N	R		O
2	K	I				A		N	
3	F			K	R				
4		K	F	N	S		O	G	
5	R	N				I	F		
6					K			R	A
7				R			A	F	
8	S				N		G		R
9	O		A		G	F		I	

Hint: Column E

What the wayward Israelites confessed doing to the Lord: _____ Him. (Judges 10:10)

PUZZLE 12

For A7, D2, G3, I6
"Lo, ___ born in my house is mine heir." (Genesis 15:3)

For E4, F8, I3
How many hundred shekels did Abraham pay for the burial cave? (Genesis 23:16)

For A1, D5, E3, F7, I2
On which day of creation did dry land appear? (Genesis 1:9–13)

For B2, F3, H4, I9
How many of his officers did Pharaoh put in prison? (Genesis 40:2–3)

For A2, D3, E7, F4
Which verse of Psalm 19 says, "The law of the LORD is perfect, converting the soul"?

For C3, E8, F1, G9
How many thousand camels did Job have in his latter life? (Job 42:12)

For E1, G2, I7
"Give a portion to seven, and also to ___." (Ecclesiastes 11:2)

For B8, I5
Hezekiah "reigned ___ and twenty years in Jerusalem." (2 Chronicles 29:1)

For A8, F2, H9, I1
How many trees were the Amorite kings of Joshua's time hanged on? (Joshua 10:26)

	A	B	C	D	E	F	G	H	I
1									
2									
3									
4									
5									
6									
7									
8									
9									

Starter Numbers in Order:
1, 4, 3, 2, 7, 9, 8, 6, 5

PUZZLE 13

For B6, D4, G7
What number commandment says, "Thou shalt not steal"? (Exodus 20:15)

For B1, D5
How many pillars were made for the tabernacle entrance? (Exodus 36:38)

For A5, D7, G3, H6
How many lambs did God tell Ezekiel the prince should sacrifice on the day of the new moon? (Ezekiel 46:6)

For E4
How many times was Paul beaten with rods? (2 Corinthians 11:25)

For B2, F9
How many years did Hoshea reign in Samaria? (2 Kings 17:1)

For A2, I1
In the book of Exodus, how many sheep was a convicted sheep thief to pay in restitution? (Exodus 22:1)

For D1, F8, G6
In Revelation, with how many kings is the beast associated? (Revelation 17:10–11)

For C3, F2, H4, I8
How did Moses describe "the LORD our God"? (Deuteronomy 6:4)

For A1, C4, D9
How many hours did the unruly Ephesian crowd shout its support for the goddess Diana (or Artemis)? (Acts 19:34)

	A	B	C	D	E	F	G	H	I
1									
2									
3									
4									
5									
6									
7									
8									
9									

Starter Numbers in Order:
2, 1, 7, 4, 6, 3, 9, 5, 8

PUZZLE 14

For B1, D4, H9
How many tables were to be placed on the left side of the temple? (2 Chronicles 4:8)

For C3, D7, E5, H2, I9
How many "were born to the giant in Gath, and fell by the hand of David"? (2 Samuel 21:22)

For I4
How many men were thrown into the fiery furnace? (Daniel 3:20)

For B5, C8, D2, H6
In the list of foundation stones in Revelation 21:19–20, what number is topaz?

For A7, B6, C1, F4, G8, H5
How many days did Samson give his wedding guests to solve a riddle? (Judges 14:12)

For A2, E6, H7
In the city called "The LORD is there," how many gates were named for Zebulun? (Ezekiel 48:33)

For A5, C7, D1, I3
How many Hebrew midwives were there in the time of Moses? (Exodus 1:15)

For G6
How many tables did Israel slay the sacrifices on? (Ezekiel 40:41)

For B3, D5, E7, F2, I6
During the fall of Jericho, for how many days did Joshua's armed men march once around the city? (Joshua 6:3)

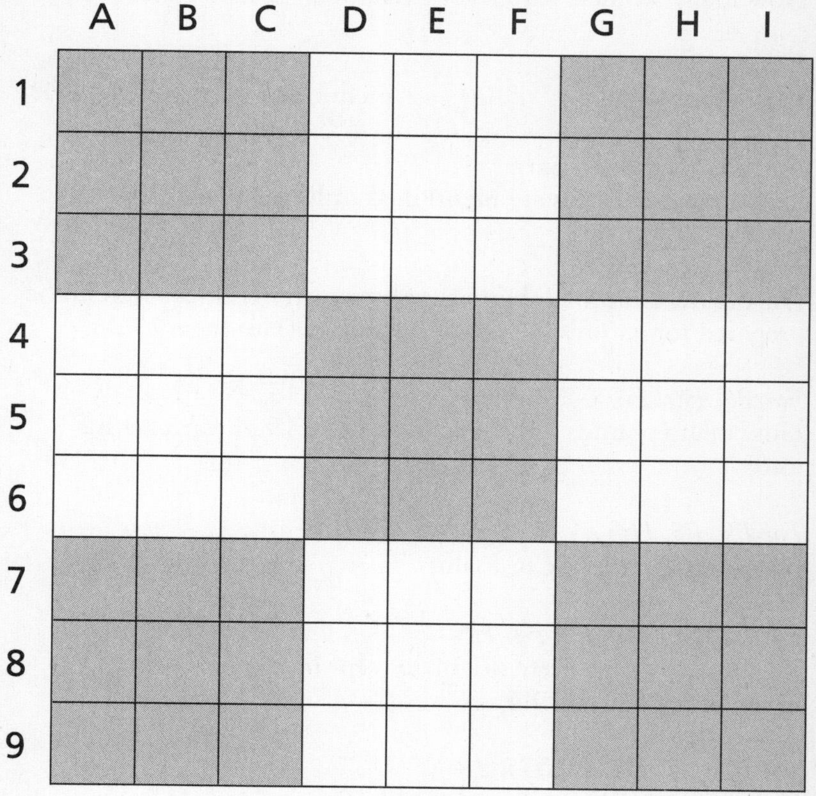

Starter Numbers in Order:

5, 4, 3, 6, 7, 1, 2, 8, 9

PUZZLE 15

For C4, D1, E5, H3
How many women bore Jacob's children? (Genesis 35:23–26)

For A9, B4, F1, I6
How many of Moses' siblings are mentioned in Numbers 12:1?

For A3, B5, C8, D7, G1
How many churches are mentioned in Revelation 1:20?

For A5, C9, G8, H6, I1
During the Feast of Tabernacles, how many bullocks were to be prepared for an offering on the fifth day? (Numbers 29:26)

For B8, D9, E6, G7
How many pounds did the man in Luke 19:18 earn for his lord?

For B9, F5, H4
How many verses are in Psalm 23?

For B2, C6, D8, E1, F4, H5
How many things were originally kept in the ark of the covenant? (Hebrews 9:4)

For B6, C7, D4, E9, G5, I8
How many books are mentioned in Revelation 5:1?

For C5, G4, H7, I2
Of the first nine chapters of Proverbs, which chapter begins, "Doth not wisdom cry?"

	A	B	C	D	E	F	G	H	I
1									
2									
3									
4									
5									
6									
7									
8									
9									

Starter Numbers in Order:
4, 2, 7, 9, 5, 6, 3, 1, 8

PUZZLE 16

For D2, F6, G3, I5
How many prophets crossed the Jordan River on dry ground before Elijah was taken to heaven? (2 Kings 2:8)

For B8, C4, E6, F9, H1
In the list of the Gadites who joined David, what number was Eliel? (1 Chronicles 12:11)

For A8, B6, D7, E4, F2, G9, H5, I1
How many months was Esther beautified with oil of myrrh? (Esther 2:12)

For C9, D8, I6
How many talents were given to the first man in this parable of Jesus? (Matthew 25:15)

For C7, D4, E2, F8, G1, H6, I9
How many days was Lazarus in the grave? (John 11:17)

For B2, C5, D6, E9, G4, H3
How many sons did Esau have with his wife Adah? (Genesis 36:4)

For D1, F7
Which seal's opening in the book of Revelation resulted in someone being given balances? (Revelation 6:5)

For A6, D5, F3, H7, I4
How many years did Abdon judge Israel? (Judges 12:13–14)

For C6, E1, G8
". . .more than over ninety and ___ just persons." (Luke 15:7)

	A	B	C	D	E	F	G	H	I
1									
2									
3									
4									
5									
6									
7									
8									
9									

Starter Numbers in Order:
2, 7, 6, 5, 4, 1, 3, 8, 9

PUZZLE 17

For A1, B7, D3, E6, H4
How many Midianite kings did the Israelites, under Moses, kill? (Numbers 31:8)

For B3, C9, F7, G8
How many heads did the huge red dragon of Revelation have? (Revelation 12:3)

For A4, B8, C3
On which day of creation did God make people? (Genesis 1:27–31)

For B4, F1, I6
On which day of creation did God make the sun and moon? (Genesis 1:16–19)

For B2, D1, F9, G6
How many days old was the Christ child when He was named "Jesus"? (Luke 2:21)

For B5, D7, E3, G2,
What number plus three was the age of Jesus when He stayed behind in Jerusalem instead of joining Mary and Joseph for the journey home? (Luke 2:42)

For D6, H1, I5
When Tabitha (or Dorcas) died, how many men were sent to get Peter in the nearby town? (Acts 9:36–38)

For A7, C6, E9, F5, H3, I8
How many nights did God warn Abimelech in a dream about Abraham's wife, Sarah? (Genesis 20:3)

For D4, E7, F3, H9, I1
What number was part of the name of the inns or taverns that Paul saw on his trip to Rome? (Acts 28:15)

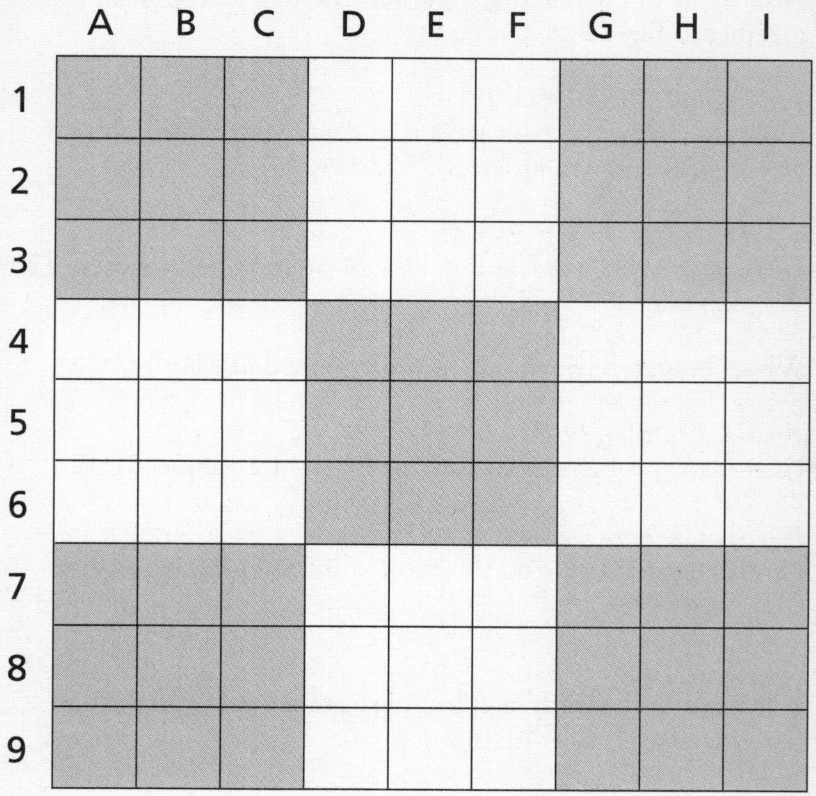

Starter Numbers in Order:
3, 1, 2, 6, 8, 4, 9, 7, 5

PUZZLE 18

For H7
How many of the tabernacle curtains were to be coupled together in Exodus 26:3?

For C9, D8, E1, F6, G3, I7
After how many days did Jesus take Peter, James, and John up on a mountain by themselves? (Matthew 17:1)

For A3, G4, I1
How many years was Jehoram king of Judah? (2 Kings 8:16–17)

For C4, F2, G8, I6
Which hour, besides the sixth, is mentioned in Matthew 20:5?

For B1, C6, E5, H9, I4
How many brothers of Goliath are listed in 2 Samuel 21:19?

For B9, C2, H4
How many seals were on the book in John's vision of heaven? (Revelation 5:1)

For A2, B5, E9
What was the breadth in cubits of the tabernacle curtains? (Exodus 26:8)

For B7, F1, G9
How many thieves were crucified with Jesus? (Matthew 27:38)

For B4, G5, H3, I9
How many sons did Noah beget? (Genesis 5:32)

	A	B	C	D	E	F	G	H	I
1									
2									
3									
4									
5									
6									
7									
8									
9									

Starter Numbers in Order:
5, 6, 8, 9, 1, 7, 4, 2, 3

PUZZLE 19

For A8, B3, D7, H6
"Let us not therefore judge ___ another any more."
(Romans 14:13)

For A1, D9, F6, G8
How many chapters are in the book of Habakkuk?

For B8, C3, D4, E9, G7, H1
Of the lots cast for temple duty, what number lot fell to Mattaniah? (1 Chronicles 25:16)

For A3, B9, C5, E6, F1, H7, I2
How many hundred years did Lamech live after he had Noah?
(Genesis 5:30)

For B7, E8, G6, H3, I9
How many measures of barley did Boaz give Ruth? (Ruth 3:15)

For A4, F7, G3, H9
In John 1:35–37, how many disciples of John the Baptist went and followed Jesus?

For D6, E7, F3
How many faces did each of the living creatures have?
(Ezekiel 1:5–6)

For F9, H8, I3
How many days old was a male child to be when he was circumcised? (Genesis 17:12)

For B6, C1, D3, E5, H4
Which verse of Philippians 4 says that the peace of God passes all understanding?

	A	B	C	D	E	F	G	H	I
1									
2									
3									
4									
5									
6									
7									
8									
9									

Starter Numbers in Order:
1, 3, 9, 5, 6, 2, 4, 8, 7

PUZZLE 20

	A	B	C	D	E	F	G	H	I
1		S			G		R	A	
2	D		R	P					E
3	G			I				D	
4	A	R	I	S		P	G		
5					A	R			D
6			E		I	G	A	S	
7			G	R				O	A
8		A	O		E			I	
9		P				S	E	R	

Hint: Column C

We should continually offer the sacrifice of ______ to ___. (Hebrews 13:15)

PUZZLE 21

	A	B	C	D	E	F	G	H	I
1		T	I	O		G			Y
2	O				E			T	
3	Y		M	I					N
4	G			E		Y			
5		Y		N	M	O	T		G
6			O	H		T		N	
7		M			Y	I			
8			G			E	N		M
9	T	H		M	O			G	I

Hint: Column G

A title for Jesus: _______ ___ of Jacob. (Isaiah 60:16)

PUZZLE 22

For A9, F1, I6
How many princes of the Midianites did Gideon's army slay? (Judges 7:25)

For B5, D6, H3
Of the oxen holding up the molten sea at Solomon's temple, how many faced in each direction? (2 Chronicles 4:4)

For A1, C6, F5, I7
How many times was the blood sprinkled before the Lord? (Leviticus 4:6)

For B2, C5, E3, H8
". . .every ___ after his tongue. . ." (Genesis 10:5)

For C3, F2
". . .___ hundred and fifty and six." (1 Chronicles 9:9)

For G9, H6
How many paces did the ark go before the sacrifice was made? (2 Samuel 6:13)

For C8, D1, E4, F9, H5, I3
How many hundred pomegranates were on the two wreaths on the temple's pillars? (2 Chronicles 4:13)

For B1, D8, F3
How many hundred years old was Noah when he had his children? (Genesis 5:32)

For A4, B7, C2, E8, H9
In the first nine psalms, which psalm begins, "O LORD our Lord, how excellent is thy name in all the earth!"?

	A	B	C	D	E	F	G	H	I
1									
2									
3									
4									
5									
6									
7									
8									
9									

Starter Numbers in Order:
2, 3, 7, 1, 9, 6, 4, 5, 8

PUZZLE 23

For A1, C7, D6, E3
How many years could one have a Hebrew slave serve them? (Jeremiah 34:14)

For B1, D4, E9, H7
How many languages did the world's people speak when they started building the tower of Babel? (Genesis 11:1–9)

For A6, D3, G9
How many sons did Jesse have? (1 Samuel 17:12)

For E1, I5
How many thousand people were killed in Revelation's earthquake in Jerusalem? (Revelation 11:13)

For A2, F1, G7, I3
How many thousand men did Joshua use to ambush enemies near Ai? (Joshua 8:10–12)

For A8, C2, E7, G1, I4
What number in the list of the fruit of the Spirit is joy? (Galatians 5:22–23)

For A4, C9, E5, F7, G2, H6
In Jesus' parable, how many years had a fig tree produced no fruit before its owner threatened to cut it down? (Luke 13:7)

For B8, C6, E4, G5, H1
How many months (plus twenty days) did it take Joab to make a census of Israel and Judah? (2 Samuel 24:2, 8)

For A9, B4, C3, D7, H8, I1
How many rows of stones were on the breastplate of judgment? (Exodus 28:15–17)

	A	B	C	D	E	F	G	H	I
1									
2									
3									
4									
5									
6									
7									
8									
9									

Starter Numbers in Order:
6, 1, 8, 7, 5, 2, 3, 9, 4

PUZZLE 24

For A4
How many years was Joash hidden in the house of God? (2 Chronicles 22:11–12)

For A9, D3, F6
How many living creatures are described in Ezekiel 1:5?

For C9, D8, H4
How many trumpets are mentioned in Revelation 8:2?

For B9, C3, F7, I4
How many loaves did Jesus miraculously multiply into a dinner for five thousand people? (Matthew 14:17)

For C2, H1
How many bullocks are mentioned in Numbers 29:26?

For D2, H3
How many soldiers pierced Jesus' side with a spear? (John 19:34)

For B6, C1, G2
In Matthew 23:13, how many groups did Jesus pronounce woes upon?

For B2, D4, G7
How many wives did Esau have? (Genesis 36:2–3)

For E4, I2
How many oxen did Moses give to the sons of Merari? (Numbers 7:8)

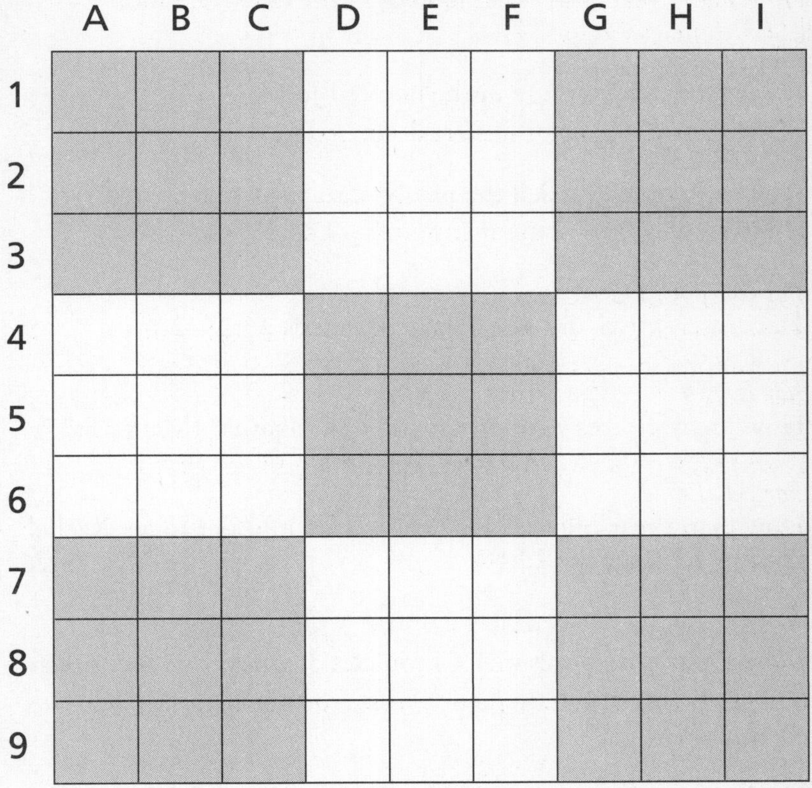

Starter Numbers in Order:
6, 4, 7, 5, 9, 1, 2, 3, 8

PUZZLE 25

For A2, F9, G5, H7
How many sons did Leah have? (Genesis 30:20)

For B7, D2, H5
How many chapters are in the book of Jude?

For A7, C3
How many men carried the paralytic to Jesus to be cured? (Mark 2:3)

For D4, G7, H3
How many wives did Jacob have? (Genesis 29:23–28)

For E7, I4
How many crosses were on the hill of Golgotha? (Mark 15:27)

For B1, D9, I2
How many years did Jacob agree to serve in order to get Rachel as his wife? (Genesis 29:18)

For B5, F2
Of the first nine verses in 1 Chronicles 3, which one mentions David's daughter?

For C4, D1, G8
How many pillars were made for the hanging in the tabernacle? (Exodus 26:37)

For A6, E4, G9
What number times five equals the days and nights Jesus fasted before meeting Satan? (Matthew 4:1–2)

	A	B	C	D	E	F	G	H	I
1									
2									
3									
4									
5									
6									
7									
8									
9									

Starter Numbers in Order:
6, 1, 4, 2, 3, 7, 9, 5, 8

PUZZLE 26

	A	B	C	D	E	F	G	H	I
1	H			B				E	A
2		B	E			A	F		H
3	A	D			H				
4	F				B	E			R
5		I		D	S			A	
6	D			F	R			S	B
7					D			H	
8	E		B	S			I		D
9	I	A				R			S

Hint: Column D

Jesus multiplied ______ and _____ in His miracle.
(Matthew 14:19)

PUZZLE 27

	A	B	C	D	E	F	G	H	I
1	T	R		S			I	B	
2	I			R			H	O	
3	B		N	E		I		R	
4	S				R			N	
5	O	E		B			T	I	
6	H				T		E		
7		I	S		E	H		T	B
8			O			R			
9	R	H		N			O		S

Hint: Column H

Line of lyrics from the popular Christmas hymn "The First Noel": _____ __ ____ King of Israel. (Matthew 2:2)

PUZZLE 28

For C1, E5, H9
How many escaped Lot's kidnappers to report to Abram what had happened? (Genesis 14:12–13)

For A2, B8, D1, E7, F4
How many Amorite kings joined forces to attack the city of Gibeon? (Joshua 10:5)

For D6, E2, G5, H3
In Revelation, how many thunders did the voice of an angel sound like? (Revelation 10:1, 3)

For B2, D5, F1, H8, I4
How many days had a multitude been with Jesus before He fed them? (Mark 8:2)

For A5, F3, G7
What number results from subtracting the number of horsemen in Revelation from the number of Jesus' disciples? (Revelation 6:1–8; Matthew 10:1)

For A4, C8, E6, F9, G1
How many wagons or carts were given to the Merari Levites for their service with the tabernacle? (Numbers 7:8)

For B5, C3, G2, I9
What number plus 3 equals the number of Jesus' apostles? (Matthew 10:2)

For A9, E3, H1, I8
How many possible replacements for Judas Iscariot did the eleven apostles test by lot? (Acts 1:23–25)

For B7, C6, D9, H5, I1
In Isaiah's vision, how many wings did each seraphim have? (Isaiah 6:2)

	A	B	C	D	E	F	G	H	I
1									
2									
3									
4									
5									
6									
7									
8									
9									

Starter Numbers in Order:

1, 5, 7, 3, 8, 4, 9, 2, 6

PUZZLE 29

For A4, F5, H7, I6
How many debtors are mentioned in Luke 7:41?

For E7, F2, G6, H1, I9
Of the first nine psalms, which one begins, "Blessed is the man that walketh not in the counsel of the ungodly"?

For B6, D4
How many days were the men of war to march once around the city of Jericho? (Joshua 6:3)

For B5, F3
How many cubits was the wing of one cherub in the most holy house in Solomon's temple? (2 Chronicles 3:10–11)

For B7, C5, E3, F8, G2
How many chapters are in the book of Jonah?

For A8, C4, D1, F9, H6
According to 1 Samuel 17:12, how many sons did Jesse have?

For B1, F4, H8, I5
How many stars are mentioned in Revelation 1:20?

For D9, E4
How many sons did David's sister Zeruiah have?
(1 Chronicles 2:16)

For E2, F6, G4, H3
What number times 100 was the number of iron chariots belonging to Sisera? (Judges 4:2–3)

	A	B	C	D	E	F	G	H	I
1									
2									
3									
4									
5									
6									
7									
8									
9									

Starter Numbers in Order:
2, 1, 6, 5, 4, 8, 7, 3, 9

PUZZLE 30

	A	B	C	D	E	F	G	H	I
1		O		C	H	I	N	T	A
2	I				R			H	
3				O			C		
4	A	N							H
5	S				O	C		N	
6	C		I	H				S	
7		I	N		C				
8	O			N	I		T		C
9			C	R				I	

Hint: Row 4

__ ________ is considered a very foolish bird in the Bible. (Job 39:13–17)

PUZZLE 31

	A	B	C	D	E	F	G	H	I
1		H				W		N	
2			O			G	W	H	T
3	N		G	I					
4	H			W	E			G	
5			T	H	G			I	
6			L					E	W
7	L		I		W		E	T	
8		N	W		I			L	O
9	O			G			N		

Hint: Row 1

___ ______ kine carried the captured ark back to Israel.
(1 Samuel 6:12)

PUZZLE 32

For A5, C8, D3, E6, H9
In the list of Jesse's sons in 1 Chronicles 2:13–15, which number son is Raddai?

For A6, C3, F9
How many months was Jehoahaz king of Judah? (2 Kings 23:31)

For B2
How many Gospels are there in the New Testament?

For D1, H6, I7
How many angels came from the east in Revelation 7:2?

For A9, F1, G7
How many daughters-in-law did Naomi have? (Ruth 1:4)

For G4, H3, I8
On what day did God rest? (Genesis 2:3)

For D2
How many chapters are in the book of 1 Timothy?

For A3, E8
How many years was Hoshea king of Israel? (2 Kings 17:1)

For C2, F4, G5, H7
What number times 5 was the number of years Saul son of Cis ruled Israel? (Acts 13:21)

	A	B	C	D	E	F	G	H	I
1									
2									
3									
4									
5									
6									
7									
8									
9									

Starter Numbers in Order:
5, 3, 4, 1, 2, 7, 6, 9, 8

PUZZLE 33

For A1, C7, F4, I3
In John's Revelation, how many angels stood before God? (Revelation 8:2)

For A8, B2, C5, E4, F9, H7
How many swords did the disciples find on the night of Jesus' arrest? (Luke 22:38)

For B3, D4, E8, I5
According to the prophet Amos, how many months away from harvest did the Lord threaten to withhold rain from idolatrous Israel? (Amos 4:7)

For B4, C1, D9, G8, H5
What kind of "flesh" is there when a man cleaves unto his wife? (Genesis 2:24)

For A6, B7, E2, H4
After Joshua died, how many Philistine rulers did God leave to teach warfare to the Israelites? (Judges 3:2–3)

For A4, B9, C2, E5, F1, H3
After his personal tragedy, how many thousand camels was Job blessed with? (Job 42:12)

For E3, G1, H9, I4
On what day of his young life was John the Baptist circumcised? (Luke 1:59–60)

For C4, G2, H6, I9
How many feet characterized the flying insects the Israelites were forbidden to eat? (Leviticus 11:23)

For E7, G4
How many hundred iron chariots did Sisera have to oppose Deborah's army? (Judges 4:1–4)

	A	B	C	D	E	F	G	H	I
1									
2									
3									
4									
5									
6									
7									
8									
9									

Starter Numbers in Order:
7, 2, 3, 1, 5, 9, 8, 4, 6

PUZZLE 34

For A1, B5, F7, H4
How many weeks passed in which Daniel ate no meat after his vision of a man? (Daniel 10:3–5)

For A9, B2, C6, E3, G8, H5
How many days per year did Israel's daughters lament Jephthah's daughter? (Judges 11:40)

For A8, C3, E9, G5, I7
How many choice sheep were prepared for Governor Nehemiah each day? (Nehemiah 5:18)

For D9, E1, H8
What number times 10 was the age of Sarah when she was told she would bear Isaac? (Genesis 17:15–17)

For C7, E2, G9, I4
How many men did Joseph's ten brothers say fathered them? (Genesis 42:11)

For A5, F2, I6
How old was Josiah when he became king of Judah? (2 Chronicles 34:1)

For C4, D6, E8, G1, H9, I5
How many seals are on the book to be opened by the Lion of the tribe of Judah? (Revelation 5:5)

For B9, C5, D4, E7, G2
When the Son of man is revealed, how many women will be grinding when one is taken? (Luke 17:30, 35)

For E5, I2
How many warriors did the Danites send to spy out the land of Laish? (Judges 18:2)

	A	B	C	D	E	F	G	H	I
1									
2									
3									
4									
5									
6									
7									
8									
9									

Starter Numbers in Order:
3, 4, 6, 9, 1, 8, 7, 2, 5

PUZZLE 35

For A4, C8, D5, E2, G6, H3
In Pharaoh's dream, how many kine were "fatfleshed and well favoured"? (Genesis 41:18)

For B4, C7, G5
How many chapters are in the book of Haggai?

For C9, D7, E5, G8
Which verse of Psalm 100 says, "We are his people, and the sheep of his pasture"?

For B9, D1, H2, I6
How many lepers returned to thank Jesus after He cleansed them? (Luke 17:15–17)

For C1, D3, F5
On what day after His birth was Jesus named? (Luke 2:21)

For C5, D6, I1
How many chief porters were at the temple? (1 Chronicles 9:26)

For B7, C4, D2, F8, G3
In what chapter of Luke does Herod admit to having beheaded John the Baptist?

For A3, B8, C6, D4, H1
How many years were the Israelites to sow their land? (Exodus 23:10)

For F3, G1
The altar in Exodus 27:1 was how many cubits long?

	A	B	C	D	E	F	G	H	I
1									
2									
3									
4									
5									
6									
7									
8									
9									

Starter Numbers in Order:
7, 2, 3, 1, 8, 4, 9, 6, 5

PUZZLE 36

	A	B	C	D	E	F	G	H	I
1		S	I	O	T	U		E	R
2			U					T	I
3		O		R				U	
4	I			E		G			H
5		E		U	S		I		
6					H			S	E
7		U	H	S	G		T		
8	S	R					E		
9				H	U		G	R	

Hint: Column I

God saw Noah was this before him: ___________.
(Genesis 7:1)

PUZZLE 37

	A	B	C	D	E	F	G	H	I
1		F	C				A	M	U
2		A	L	C		U			
3	E				A				C
4			F			A	R		
5			E	R				U	L
6	U		I		M			E	
7	L		R	I			E		F
8		U	A		R				I
9	I				L				R

Hint: Row 5

The Lord thy God is _ ________ God. (Deuteronomy 4:31)

PUZZLE 38

For A1, E5, F8, G9, I3
How many times a day did Daniel's enemies accuse him of praying? (Daniel 6:13)

For A4, B1, D9, G8
How many cherubs were to be made on each end of the mercy seat? (Exodus 25:19)

For A7, B2, C5, H6, I9
How many stars were held by the One who addressed Sardis? (Revelation 3:1)

For B4, C1, F6, H5, I7
How many months did Benjamites, fleeing from Israel's army, stay at Rimmon's rock? (Judges 20:46–47)

For B5, C9, D4, E2
How many cities were given to the descendants of Aaron? (Joshua 21:13–16)

For C8, F1, I2,
How many blind men sat by the wayside as Jesus passed through Jericho? (Matthew 20:29–30)

For F9, G3
How many years did young Joash stay hidden from his grandmother Athaliah at the temple of God? (2 Chronicles 22:10–12)

For E8, H2, I4
What number plus 30 was the number of years that the man by the Bethesda pool had an infirmity? (John 5:5)

For B9, D7, E4, F3, I1
How many sheep did Abigail, wife of the foolish Nabal, give to David and his men? (1 Samuel 25:18–20)

	A	B	C	D	E	F	G	H	I
1									
2									
3									
4									
5									
6									
7									
8									
9									

Starter Numbers in Order:
5, 8, 9, 2, 6, 4, 7, 1, 3

PUZZLE 39

For A4, G6
In the list of the Ten Commandments, what number commandment says, "Thou shalt not steal"? (Exodus 20:15)

For A2, D3
How many chapters are in the book of Amos?

For B7, E3
How many times did Sanballat send messages to Nehemiah, asking if they could meet? (Nehemiah 6:5)

For E7, F1
How many years was Abijam king of Judah? (1 Kings 15:1–2)

For A5, C7, F8, H3
How many days was the ancient feast described in Numbers 29:12?

For A9, I3
In the list of the plagues that God visited on Egypt, what number was frogs? (Exodus 8:1–15)

For C3, E4, H2
In what year of Solomon's reign did he begin to build the house of the Lord? (1 Kings 6:1)

For E6, F2, G7
How many chapters are in the book of 3 John?

For B5, D7, F6, G1
How many water pots were at the wedding at Cana? (John 2:1, 6)

	A	B	C	D	E	F	G	H	I
1									
2									
3									
4									
5									
6									
7									
8									
9									

Starter Numbers in Order:
8, 9, 5, 3, 7, 2, 4, 1, 6

PUZZLE 40

For A3, D5, E8, G4
During the siege of Samaria, how many pieces of silver did a fourth part of a cab of dove dung cost? (2 Kings 6:25)

For B1, D4, G9, H3
How many tribes (plus half a tribe) were to receive land allotments west of the Jordan? (Joshua 14:2–3)

For B2, E9, H5
How many staves did the prophet Zechariah use to pasture the flock marked for slaughter? (Zechariah 11:7)

For B3, D7, I4
According to God, how many lambs were the ancient Israelites to sacrifice each morning? (Exodus 29:39)

For A9, B5, D2, G6
Besides Noah, how many other people did God save during the flood? (2 Peter 2:5)

For A6, E5, F1, I7
How many gates will be on the north side of the city called "The Lord is there"? (Ezekiel 48:31, 35)

For B7, C4, E3, G1, H6, I8
How many steps led up to King Solomon's throne? (2 Chronicles 9:18)

For B4, D6, F3, G2
Ultimately, how many sons of Gath's giant died by the hands of David and his men? (2 Samuel 21:22)

For B8, H7, I2
After reaching the porch on the eighth day, how many more days did Hezekiah's priests need to consecrate the temple? (2 Chronicles 29:17)

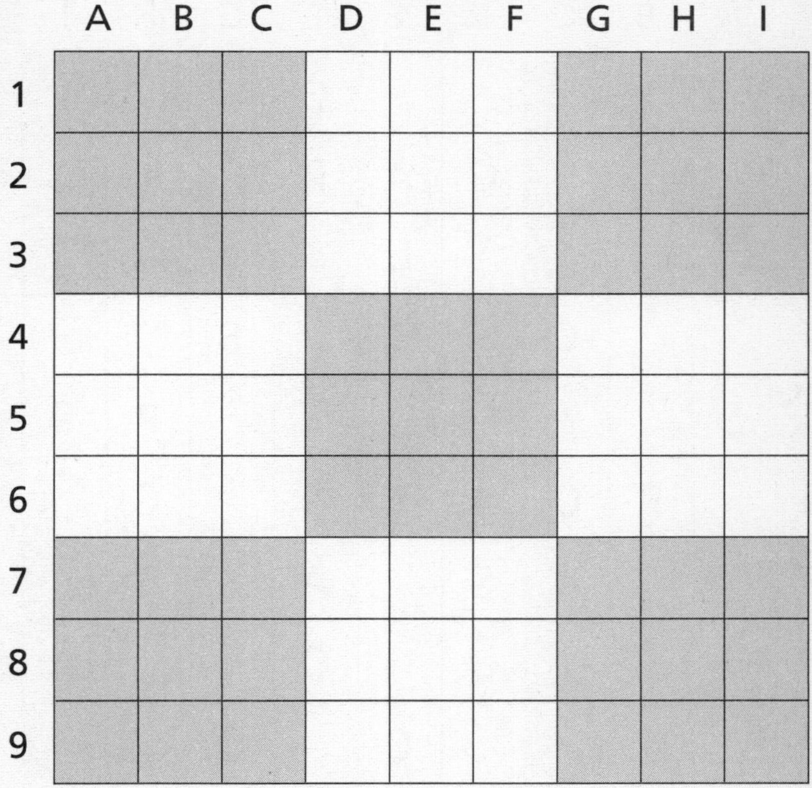

Starter Numbers in Order:
5, 6, 2, 1, 7, 3, 9, 4, 8

PUZZLE 41

	A	B	C	D	E	F	G	H	I
1			P			C	U		
2		S		O	A	R	P	I	C
3			I		U				
4			C		E		S		
5	S							R	P
6		R	O	A	I	S		C	
7			U	S		A		E	
8		I		U		O			A
9	A	P			C		O		

Hint: Row 9

Leah called her sixth son _ ________ gift.
(Genesis 30:20 NIV)

	A	B	C	D	E	F	G	H	I
1	D	E	F			W	O		
2					D	N		F	
3	R		L						U
4	N			E			D		
5		D		R	F	O	U		
6		U		N	W		L	R	
7		O				R			L
8	F		E		U		N	W	
9		L				F	R	E	

Hint: Row 7

A name Isaiah foretold Jesus would have: __________.
(Isaiah 9:6)

PUZZLE 43

For C4, D9, F6, G2
Which verse of 1 Corinthians 13 says that "love never fails"(NIV)?

For A3, F1, I2
How many sons did Joseph have? (Genesis 48:1)

For B2, G1, I8
How many generations were there between Enoch and Shem? (Hint: Do not count Enoch and Shem.) (Genesis 5:19–32)

For C2, D3, G7, H4
In what chapter of Acts does Peter visit the saints in Lydda?

For B6, C1, F9, H2
How many priests were to lead the Israelites around Jericho on the last day of their march? (Joshua 6:4)

For C5, D2, F7, G3, I6
The widow whose oil and flour were multiplied had how many sons? (1 Kings 17:12–16)

For D7, F2, I5
David reigned in Hebron for seven years and how many months? (1 Chronicles 3:4)

For B4, F8, I3
In the story of the rich man and Lazarus, how many brethren did the rich man have? (Luke 16:28)

For A2, C8, D1
How many thousand stalls did Solomon have for horses and chariots? (2 Chronicles 9:25)

	A	B	C	D	E	F	G	H	I
1									
2									
3									
4									
5									
6									
7									
8									
9									

Starter Numbers in Order:
4, 5, 9, 1, 7, 6, 3, 2, 8

PUZZLE 44

For A2, B5, D9, E3, G4
What number commandment says, "Thou shalt not bear false witness against thy neighbour"? (Exodus 20:16)

For A4, C3, I9
How many days did Paul stay with the disciples in Tyre? (Acts 21:3–4)

For A8, C6, F7, H9
How many barrels of water were poured onto Elijah's sacrifice? (1 Kings 18:31–33)

For B7, D1, F8, I3
How many hundred thousand warriors did Jeroboam use against Abijah's force? (2 Chronicles 13:3)

For A9, D5, E7, H8
In the Lord's illustration to Amos, how many sheep legs can be saved from the lion's mouth? (Amos 3:12)

For B3, E1, G2, H5, I7
With the birth of Zebulun, how many sons did Jacob have with Leah? (Genesis 30:19–20)

For A7, D4, E2, I5
For the first passover, how many lambs were sacrificed per household? (Exodus 12:3, 11)

For B4, F5, G3
In Old Testament law, how many shekels was the redemption price of every firstborn son? (Numbers 18:15–16)

For A3, G7, H1
How many years was Isaiah commanded to go naked and barefoot as a sign? (Isaiah 20:3)

	A	B	C	D	E	F	G	H	I
1									
2									
3									
4									
5									
6									
7									
8									
9									

Starter Numbers in Order:
3, 5, 1, 9, 2, 8, 4, 7, 6

PUZZLE 45

For C1, E5, G7, H6
How many sons did Zilpah have? (Genesis 30:10–12)

For D8, G1, I5
How many fringes were the ancient Israelites to wear on their vestures? (Deuteronomy 22:12)

For B2, C8, D6, H4
How many years, plus six months, did David reign in Hebron? (1 Chronicles 3:4)

For A7, C6, I9
Of the first nine chapters of Genesis, which chapter says in verse 4 that there were giants in the earth?

For C9, D3, H1
In which verse of Jude does Michael the archangel tell the devil, "The Lord rebuke thee"?

For B1, C5, D7, F4
On which day of creation did God name the dry land "Earth"? (Genesis 1:10–13)

For B5
The sounding of which angel in Revelation results in hail and fire? (Revelation 8:7)

For B7, C4, E9, F2, H3
How many chapters are in the book of James?

For D9, F5, G4, H8, I2
What number plus 76 was the age of Anna the prophetess when she beheld the baby Jesus? (Luke 2:37)

	A	B	C	D	E	F	G	H	I
1									
2									
3									
4									
5									
6									
7									
8									
9									

Starter Numbers in Order:
2, 4, 7, 6, 9, 3, 1, 5, 8

PUZZLE 46

	A	B	C	D	E	F	G	H	I
1	S			T		D		G	
2							D		H
3	U		I		G	S			O
4	D	I	S					W	
5			T		O	I		H	
6			H			W			G
7						H			W
8	G		D		I		H		
9	H	S	W			U			I

Hint: Row 8

Immanuel means this: ___ ____ __.
(Matthew 1:23)

PUZZLE 47

	A	B	C	D	E	F	G	H	I
1	B	P		U				I	A
2			N	I	B				L
3		A			P			S	
4		L			S	N	I	U	
5		I		A			P		C
6		U	B				A		
7	C					I		B	
8		S	A			P			
9				N	C	U			P

Hint: Row 6

Another word for tax collectors: __________.
(Matthew 9:11)

PUZZLE 48

For A2, D9
In Ezekiel 1:17, how many directions (or "sides") are mentioned?

For A3, B9, D1
The pouring out of which angel's vial of wrath resulted in the river Euphrates drying up? (Revelation 16:12)

For A8, E6, G7
Of the first nine chapters in Isaiah, which chapter contains in verse 14 the prophecy that a virgin shall conceive and bear a son?

For A1
In the list of Jesse's sons, which number son is Shimea? (1 Chronicles 2:13–15)

For C3, E7, H8
Of the first nine chapters in Genesis, which chapter contains the genealogy from Seth to Shem, Ham, and Japheth?

For B6, D4, H1
How many souls does Peter say were saved by water in the time of Noah? (1 Peter 3:20)

For A4, E5, F8, I9
Of the four beasts that surround the throne, which one resembles a lion? (Revelation 4:7)

For C8, E1, G5
How many farthings did Jesus say were given for five sparrows? (Luke 12:6)

For G6, I2
In the first nine chapters of Isaiah, which chapter contains in verse 7 the promise that God's kingdom will last forever?

	A	B	C	D	E	F	G	H	I
1									
2									
3									
4									
5									
6									
7									
8									
9									

Starter Numbers in Order:
4, 6, 7, 3, 5, 8, 1, 2, 9

PUZZLE 49

For A3, B4, C8, D6
How many sons did the Jewish chief priest Sceva have? (Acts 19:14)

For B1, D7, F4, I8
How many years did Hoshea reign as king of Israel? (2 Kings 17:1)

For B2, D4, E8
How many sons of Michal did King David hand over to the Gibeonites? (2 Samuel 21:8–9)

For B7, C1, G9, H2
How many sons did Noah have? (Genesis 5:32)

For B9, D1, F5, I2
How many Levites were on guard each day at the east gate of the temple? (1 Chronicles 26:17)

For C6, F1, G4
Jesus said if someone compels you to go one mile, how many should you go? (Matthew 5:41)

For E3, G1, H8
How many daughters of Putiel did Aaron's son Eleazar marry? (Exodus 6:25)

For B6, D8, H5
How many sons did Issachar have? (1 Chronicles 7:1)

For A8, E6, F9, G5, I1
What number plus 10 equals those who died when the tower in Siloam fell, as related by Jesus? (Luke 13:4)

	A	B	C	D	E	F	G	H	I
1									
2									
3									
4									
5									
6									
7									
8									
9									

Starter Numbers in Order:
8, 4, 1, 2, 9, 3, 5, 6, 7

PUZZLE 50

	A	B	C	D	E	F	G	H	I
1		V		I			E		
2	R				N			V	A
3	S		E		Y			D	
4				Y		S		A	D
5		Y		N	A	R	V		
6			N		D	V	S		
7	E		I		S	N	D	Y	
8				R			I		S
9	Y			D	E			N	R

Hint: Column B

The Israelites accused Moses of not giving them their inheritance of fields and __________. (Numbers 16:14)

PUZZLE 51

	A	B	C	D	E	F	G	H	I
1		H		R		I	N		
2		R		N	O				G
3		E			H			R	S
4		I			E	R		S	N
5			O		I	H	E		
6		S				G			
7	S	O		E			G		
8		G	E	H		S	B	N	
9			N			O			

Hint: Row 3

Whose house, wife, things, etc., we are not to covet: ________.
(Exodus 20:17 NIV)

PUZZLE 52

For B8, C6, F9, H5, I7
The sounding of which angel's trumpet resulted in someone getting the key to the bottomless pit? (Revelation 9:1)

For D5, I4
How many daughters did King Saul have? (1 Samuel 18:17–20)

For B1, E5, G2, I8
In the nine chapters of the book of Amos, which chapter says in verse 3 that two cannot walk together unless they agree?

For C4, E3, F5, I6
What, according to the King James Version, was the temple's hour of prayer? (Acts 3:1)

For E2
How old was Josiah when he became king of Judah? (2 Chronicles 34:1)

For A7, G8
In the list of the Ten Commandments, what number commands us to remember the sabbath day? (Exodus 20:8)

For B7, D9, F3, H8
Of the first nine chapters in Revelation, which chapter begins with the opening of the seals?

For A9, B3, H7
On what day of creation was the first evening and morning? (Genesis 1:5)

For A8, B6, C3, D4, E7, H1
How many years was Ibzan judge of Israel? (Judges 12:8–9)

	A	B	C	D	E	F	G	H	I
1									
2									
3									
4									
5									
6									
7									
8									
9									

Starter Numbers in Order:
5, 2, 3, 9, 8, 4, 6, 1, 7

PUZZLE 53

For A1, B9, C5, H3
How many years did King Jehoram reign in Jerusalem? (2 Kings 8:16–17)

For A4, E5, I9
How many smooth stones did David pick from the brook? (1 Samuel 17:40)

For A9, B3, C6, D5
How many people did Moses murder? (Exodus 2:12)

For D1, E7, H4
How many sons did Jeduthun have? (1 Chronicles 25:3)

For C3, D9, E1, G7
On what day of creation did God make the stars? (Genesis 1:16–19)

For A8, E2, F7, H5
In the parable of the good shepherd, how many sheep plus 90 do not wander off? (Matthew 18:13)

For C7, G1, H8
How many raiding bands did the Chaldeans form against Job's camels? (Job 1:17)

For B4, F6, G2, I5
How many nations in Canaan did God help the Israelites destroy? (Acts 13:19)

For C8, D4, E9, G5, I1
How many people on earth need to agree about something for God to answer their prayer? (Matthew 18:19)

	A	B	C	D	E	F	G	H	I
1									
2									
3									
4									
5									
6									
7									
8									
9									

Starter Numbers in Order:
2, 7, 3, 6, 4, 9, 1, 5, 8

PUZZLE 54

For B4, E1, G9
The opening of which number seal resulted in a red horse being revealed? (Revelation 6:3–4)

For F3
How many chapters are in the book of Nahum?

For A1, C7, E9, G5
How many winds are mentioned in Matthew 24:31?

For A9, E8, F5, I7
How many kid goats were sacrificed as a sin offering to make atonement? (Numbers 29:5)

For C9
Which number seal, opened in heaven, resulted in the stars falling? (Revelation 6:12–13)

For B7, G1, H5
How many times did Paul receive thirty-nine stripes? (2 Corinthians 11:24)

For B1, D5
After how many months (and 20 days) of counting the fighting men in Israel did Joab return to Jerusalem? (2 Samuel 24:8)

For D9, E2, F6, G7
How many times did Elijah's servant go again to look for rain in the sky over the sea? (1 Kings 18:43–44)

For C5, E4, F8, H2
Of Jesse's sons, what number was David? (1 Samuel 17:12–14)

	A	B	C	D	E	F	G	H	I
1									
2									
3									
4									
5									
6									
7									
8									
9									

Starter Numbers in Order:
2, 3, 4, 1, 6, 5, 9, 7, 8

PUZZLE 55

	A	B	C	D	E	F	G	H	I
1					I		K		V
2	I			V	K	L			
3	V	K		C	S		E		L
4		L	V						C
5				T				K	
6		C	K				I	V	
7		T	L	I	V	E			
8		I	S		L			E	T
9				S	T	C			

Hint: Column A

The fifth plague was upon this: __________.
(Exodus 9:4 NIV)

PUZZLE 56

	A	B	C	D	E	F	G	H	I
1				G	R	E			
2		A	D	T		N	H		
3		R		H			E		N
4	G			E		R	D		O
5	N					T	R		G
6		D				G		T	
7			H	D		O	G		
8		G				A			
9		E		R				A	D

Hint: Column G

Michael and his angels fought against ___ ______.
(Revelation 12:7)

PUZZLE 57

For A1, C6, H8
How many fingers did a huge man from Gath, a descendant of Rapha, have on each hand? (1 Chronicles 20:6)

For B2, F8, H7
How many of his disciples did John the Baptist send to ask Jesus some questions? (Luke 7:18–19)

For A4, C1, E6, H3
In the census, how many hundred thousand valiant men were in Israel, not Judah? (2 Samuel 24:9)

For A8, B3, D1, E9, H5
Initially, how many of Joseph's brothers found their money in their food sack? (Genesis 42:27)

For A5, C7, D3, E8, G6
How many strands make a cord "not quickly broken"? (Ecclesiastes 4:12)

For D8, F1, H4, I3
How many brothers were in the Sadducees' trick question to Jesus? (Luke 20:27–33)

For B9, D5, F2
On what day of creation did fowl fly across the earth? (Genesis 1:20–23)

For F5, H9, I6
What number plus 31 equals the number of days Ezekiel was to lie on his right side, according to God's instructions? (Ezekiel 4:6)

For B5, C9, E2, G1, I8
How many corners of Job's oldest son's house did a great wind smite? (Job 1:18–19)

	A	B	C	D	E	F	G	H	I
1									
2									
3									
4									
5									
6									
7									
8									
9									

Starter Numbers in Order:
4, 6, 5, 7, 3, 1, 8, 2, 9

PUZZLE 58

For C7, D6, E8
How many boards were made for the west side of the tabernacle? (Exodus 36:27)

For B1, E2, G9
Which number seal, opened in heaven, resulted in a white horse being revealed? (Revelation 6:1–2)

For A5, D9
How many parts were Jesus' garments divided into? (John 19:23)

For A2, B9, F4, H7
How many chapters are in the book of Zephaniah?

For C1, F7, G3, H5
Of the first nine chapters in Revelation, which chapter contains the angels' sounding of the fifth and sixth trumpets?

For I4
How many chapters are in the book of 1 Peter?

For B8, F5, I1
What number plus 119 equals the number of provinces King Ahasuerus ruled over from India to Ethiopia? (Esther 1:1)

For C6
How many tribes made up the kingdom of Judah? (1 Kings 12:20–21)

For D3, H8
How many times did the Shunammite's son sneeze before he opened his eyes and saw Elisha? (2 Kings 4:35–36)

	A	B	C	D	E	F	G	H	I
1									
2									
3									
4									
5									
6									
7									
8									
9									

Starter Numbers in Order:
6, 1, 4, 3, 9, 5, 8, 2, 7

PUZZLE 59

For A3, B8, D5, H9, I4
According to Old Testament law, how many years are the fields to be sown before letting the land lie still? (Exodus 23:10–11)

For A4, B1, I2
Into how many pieces will the Mount of Olives cleave when Jesus returns? (Zechariah 14:4)

For C2, G8, H4
How many years was Anna married before she became a widow? (Luke 2:36)

For C4, E2
How many years were the Israelites subject to Chushan-rishathaim? (Judges 3:8)

For A8, C5, E9, F1, H7, I6
In one of Ezekiel's visions, how many faces did each creature have? (Ezekiel 1:6)

For C8, E3, F5, G1
What number commandment says, "Honour thy father and thy mother"? (Exodus 20:12)

For B5, D6, E8, G4, I9
How many years were the bright young Jewish captives of Daniel's time to be trained in Babylon? (Daniel 1:1–5)

For A7, F8, H1
What number plus 3 equals the number of gates of pearl in the New Jerusalem? (Revelation 21:2, 21)

For D3, E7, H2
How many brothers did Joseph jail while the rest went back home? (Genesis 42:19)

	A	B	C	D	E	F	G	H	I
1									
2									
3									
4									
5									
6									
7									
8									
9									

Starter Numbers in Order:
1, 6, 3, 5, 4, 8, 7, 2, 9

PUZZLE 60

	A	B	C	D	E	F	G	H	I
1			A		G	K	I		
2			G		T		A		K
3	T	K		R					L
4				T	L			K	G
5		T		D		H			A
6	K	D	L	A			T		
7	A						G		D
8	R			G					H
9			T	K	H	L		A	

Hint: Row 2

God divided _____ from ____.
(Genesis 1:4)

PUZZLE 61

	A	B	C	D	E	F	G	H	I
1	O	R			D		A		E
2			E					N	J
3	T	H		N		E		R	D
4	R		D		N				
5		J			H	O	D	A	R
6		E			T				O
7	A			R					N
8	J	N		H	E	A			T
9	E						H	O	

Hint: Column F

God ordered Joshua to cross ___ ______ River and possess the land. (Joshua 1:11)

PUZZLE 62

For B3, H7, I4
How many times were the Israelites to march around Jericho on the seventh day? (Joshua 6:4)

For C7, D6, H8
In the book of Revelation, which angel's sounding resulted in a third of the sun, moon, and stars being darkened? (Revelation 8:12)

For A9, D2, F7, G6, H3
How many chapters are in the book of 2 Thessalonians?

For A2, F8
How many years was Elah king of Israel? (1 Kings 16:8)

For A3, B7, C6, D8, F5, H2
In which year of Zedekiah's reign did Nebuchadnezzar attack Jerusalem? (2 Kings 25:1)

For A6, C1, D7
On what day of creation did God make creatures that creep on the ground? (Genesis 1:24–31)

For A7, B5, F2, I6
How many chapters are in the Song of Solomon?

For D3, G7, H4
How many pieces made up Jesus' coat? (John 19:23–24)

For C9, D5, I2
What was the height in cubits of the molten sea at Solomon's temple? (2 Chronicles 4:2)

	A	B	C	D	E	F	G	H	
1									
2									
3									
4									
5									
6									
7									
8									
9									

Starter Numbers in Order:
7, 4, 3, 2, 9, 6, 8, 1, 5

s 61 equals the number Jesus sent out to
r future visits? (Luke 10:1)

G8
years did a Hebrew slave have to work before his
ew master freed him? (Deuteronomy 15:12)

For B4, C2, D9, I3
In a vision of Ezekiel, how many wheels were by the cherubim? (Ezekiel 10:9)

For B7, D1, F6, I8
In a vision of Zechariah, how many women had wind in their wings? (Zechariah 5:9)

For B5, C8, E3, G4
How many days of hard driving, according to Jacob, would kill the animals in the flocks he presented to Esau? (Genesis 33:13)

For D5, E7, F2, H9, I6
How many kings did Joshua learn were hiding in the cave at Makkedah? (Joshua 10:17)

For A8, D3, F9, G1, H7, I5
How many "times" were to pass while Nebuchadnezzar had a beast's heart? (Daniel 4:16)

For A9, C5, H2
How many hundred years did Adam live after he had Seth? (Genesis 5:4)

For A3, H6, I2
How many men did Nebuchadnezzar think he had thrown into the fiery furnace? (Daniel 3:24)

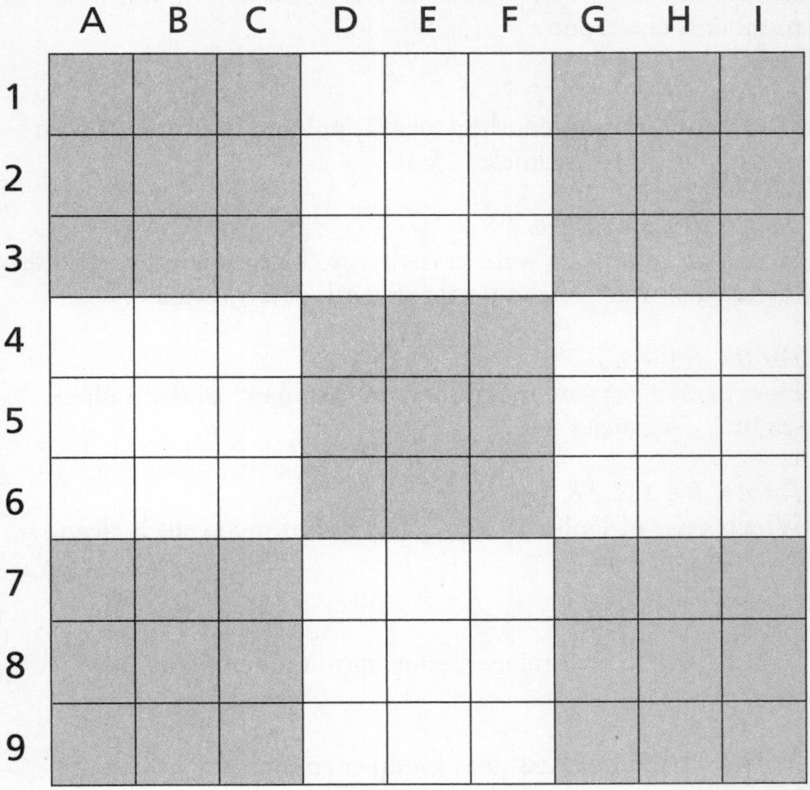

Starter Numbers in Order:
9, 6, 4, 2, 1, 5, 7, 8, 3

PUZZLE 64

For B9, C1, G3
In the foundation stones listed in Revelation 21:19–20, what number is chalcedony?

For D6, E1, F9, G8, H5
How many sons of Jeduthun were appointed to prophesy with instruments? (1 Chronicles 25:3)

For A3, B5, D8, F1, G2
How many trumpets were the priests to blow when the Israelites marched around Jericho on the seventh day? (Joshua 6:4)

For B8, E3, F5, I4
How many lavers are mentioned on each hand of the molten sea in 2 Chronicles 4:6?

For A4, B7, C2, E8, G9, 15
Which verse of Psalm 19 says, "The fear of the LORD is clean, enduring for ever"?

For D7, F3
In Luke 18:10, how many men went to the temple to pray?

For A5, F4
In what chapter of Acts does Philip encounter the Ethiopian eunuch?

For D5, E2, H9
How many sons did Abraham and Sarah have? (Genesis 21:2)

For A9, C5, H3
How many kinds of soil did Jesus describe in His parable in Matthew 13:3–9?

	A	B	C	D	E	F	G	H	I
1									
2									
3									
4									
5									
6									
7									
8									
9									

Starter Numbers in Order:
3, 6, 7, 5, 9, 2, 8, 1, 4

PUZZLE 65

	A	B	C	D	E	F	G	H	I
1	A	H	T		L				N
2	F					T	H		
3	I	D			A			L	T
4		L			D	H			
5				L	I		A	N	F
6	S	F		A	T	N			
7		N	S		F			T	
8						A			S
9	T	A	D				F	I	H

Hint: Row 8

David promised to ____ up his _____ in the Lord's name as part of his worship to God. (Psalm 63:4)

PUZZLE 66

	A	B	C	D	E	F	G	H	I
1	T			F	H			E	O
2	D	N			T	R			F
3			H	U					T
4	E		D	N			R	T	
5		H			D				U
6	R	O					F		
7				O	F	U			D
8	U	D			R	T	O		
9			F			E			R

Hint: Column I

James and John were known as the sons __ _______.
(Mark 3:17)

PUZZLE 67

For A1, D7, H3, I4
How many branches were to extend from the candlestick in the tabernacle? (Exodus 25:32)

For B1, E3
In a prophecy of Jeremiah, how many winds would be brought against Elam? (Jeremiah 49:36)

For B2, C9
How many things did the psalmist desire of the Lord? (Psalm 27:4)

For B5, D2, F4
How many oxen did Moses give to the Merari Levites? (Numbers 7:8)

For C6, E2, F7, H4, I9
How many hundred iron chariots did Sisera have? (Judges 4:13)

For A6, B7, F1, H9
How many times over would the slayer of Cain suffer vengeance? (Genesis 4:15)

For B9, E7, F5, H6
How many years after his conversion did Paul go to see Peter in Jerusalem? (Galatians 1:18)

For D9, G2
How many commandments did Jesus say the Old Testament law and prophets hang on? (Matthew 22:40)

For B6, E5, H7, I1
How many hundred years old was Noah when he had his three sons? (Genesis 5:32)

	A	B	C	D	E	F	G	H	I
1									
2									
3									
4									
5									
6									
7									
8									
9									

Starter Numbers in Order:
5, 2, 3, 7, 6, 8, 1, 4, 9

PUZZLE 68

For A7, B6, E1, G8, H3, I5
Which verse of Ecclesiastes 3 says, "A time to get, and a time to lose"?

For D1, E9
How many chapters are in the book of Philemon?

For A5, C7, D2, G3
The sounding of which angel resulted in a mountain burning with fire being thrown into the sea? (Revelation 8:8)

For B9, F7, I6
In the book of Revelation, which angel's vial of wrath resulted in the fall of the cities of the nations? (Revelation 16:17–19)

For F8, H1
In what year of Hoshea's reign over Israel was Samaria taken? (2 Kings 18:10)

For A6, G2
How many words did Paul say he would rather speak with understanding than ten thousand words in an unknown tongue? (1 Corinthians 14:19)

For B3, G7
Of the forty-eight cities given to the Levites, how many cities came from the tribe of Ephraim? (Joshua 21:20–22)

For A3, B7, F1, G6, H9
What number plus 90 was the age of Eli when he learned that his sons had both been killed? (1 Samuel 4:15–17)

For D6
What number commandment says, "Thou shalt not take the name of the LORD thy God in vain"? (Exodus 20:7)

	A	B	C	D	E	F	G	H	I
1									
2									
3									
4									
5									
6									
7									
8									
9									

Starter Numbers in Order:
6, 1, 2, 7, 9, 5, 4, 8, 3

PUZZLE 69

For A8, B5, C3, E1, F7, I4
How many horses are mentioned in 2 Kings 7:13?

For A4, B8, H7, I3
Of the forty-eight cities given to the Levites, how many cities came from the tribe of Issachar? (Joshua 21:28–29, 41)

For B3, C6, E5, F1
In the book of Revelation, which number seal resulted in someone receiving a crown? (Revelation 6:1–2)

For C1, H5, I9
Of the lots cast for temple duty, which number fell to Jeshaiah? (1 Chronicles 25:15)

For B1, D2, E4, H6, I7
Of the first nine chapters of Acts, which one records the conversion of Saul to Paul?

For G7, H1
How many sons did Azel have? (1 Chronicles 8:38)

For A3, D5, H9
Which verse in John 3 says, "Except a man be born again, he cannot see the kingdom of God"?

For B4, G6, I8
Which verse of Psalm 37 says, "Rest in the Lord, and wait patiently for him"?

For B2, D3, E7, G1
How many sons of Aaron were put to death by God? (Leviticus 10:1–2)

	A	B	C	D	E	F	G	H	I
1									
2									
3									
4									
5									
6									
7									
8									
9									

Starter Numbers in Order:
5, 4, 1, 8, 9, 6, 3, 7, 2

PUZZLE 70

	A	B	C	D	E	F	G	H	I
1	A	P			R				
2	R					U	P	C	S
3		C		S			R		
4			E			D			
5	P	U			H		S	E	
6		A			P		C	U	R
7				D		H		A	U
8		E	C		A				P
9	U	H	A				D	R	

Hint: Row 5

Abraham __________ Ephron's field and cave to bury his late wife, Sarah. (Genesis 23:16–17)

PUZZLE 71

	A	B	C	D	E	F	G	H	I
1	H	U		W		N	S		
2		W	S	U					H
3	I	N		T			U	D	
4			U	I					
5			I					U	N
6	N					O	W	I	S
7	D	T		S		U		W	
8			W					H	T
9			H			W		S	U

Hint: Column G

During Jesus' time, one knew a _____ ____ meant that it was going to be hot. (Luke 12:55)

PUZZLE 72

For A2, G5, H9
On the Day of Atonement, how many goats are used as scapegoats? (Leviticus 16:8)

For B3
How many years of famine remained when Joseph identified himself to his brothers in Egypt? (Genesis 45:4–6)

For B4
In Ezra's time, how many hundred lambs were used in the dedication sacrifice of the rebuilt temple? (Ezra 6:15, 17)

For C1, E3, F9, H7
What number plus 381 equals the number of days Ezekiel was to lie on his side, according to God's instructions? (Ezekiel 4:9)

For C5, D2, F6, G3
In the chief baker's dream, as told to Joseph, how many baskets of bread were on his head? (Genesis 40:16)

For A5, E8, F1
In a teaching of Jesus, how many masters can no one serve at the same time? (Luke 16:13)

For C8, F4
On what number day was the Sabbath? (Leviticus 23:3)

For B7, D9, G1, H4
How many sons were born to David while in Hebron? (1 Chronicles 3:1–4)

For A8, D3, G4, H2, I7
How many sons did Milcah bear to Abraham's brother Nahor? (Genesis 22:23)

	A	B	C	D	E	F	G	H	I
1									
2									
3									
4									
5									
6									
7									
8									
9									

Starter Numbers in Order:
1, 5, 4, 9, 3, 2, 7, 6, 8

PUZZLE 73

For B7, C5, G6, I9
Which verse of Ecclesiastes 3 says, "A time to love, and a time to hate"?

For A4, C2, D7, E3, F6, H5
How many daughters did Heman have? (1 Chronicles 25:5)

For C4, E9, G1
In the foundation stones listed in Revelation 21:19–20, which number is chrysolite?

For A6, B1, I7
The pouring out of which angel's vial of wrath resulted in every living soul in the sea dying? (Revelation 16:3)

For A8, B6, D1, E4, I5
Of the first nine psalms, which psalm says in verse 3, "And he shall be like a tree planted by the rivers of water"?

For C9, E7, H1
How many days before Passover did Jesus go to Bethany? (John 12:1)

For B8, D3, E6, F7, G4, I2
Of the first nine chapters in Romans, which one says in verse 8 that God commends His own love toward us?

For A1, B5, E8, F4, H6, I3
What number plus 20 was the number of years Hezekiah reigned as king of Judah? (2 Chronicles 29:1)

For B2, C6, E5, G7, H3
How many words were written on the wall by the mysterious hand and interpreted by Daniel? (Daniel 5:24–25)

	A	B	C	D	E	F	G	H	I
1									
2									
3									
4									
5									
6									
7									
8									
9									

Starter Numbers in Order:
4, 6, 5, 9, 1, 2, 7, 3, 8

PUZZLE 74

	A	B	C	D	E	F	G	H	I
1	H	S	T	N		O			G
2	G	E					N		S
3		O			G			T	H
4	O				E	S	F		
5			G		N	H	S	I	O
6									
7	F				T	N	G	E	
8		G				I		N	F
9		N	E					S	T

Hint: Row 6

We should _____ __ ___ mercies and love of the Lord forever.
(Psalm 89:1)

PUZZLE 75

	A	B	C	D	E	F	G	H	I
1		T	A	D				R	
2					H	T		G	
3	S			U		E		D	
4			R	G		U			H
5	G	U	T					E	
6	H	E	S			R		A	
7	R			E		D		T	S
8		S	D		G			U	
9			U	S	T			H	

Hint: Column D

God allowed the inheritance to go to his __________ because Zelophehad had no sons. (Numbers 27:7)

PUZZLE 76

For B1, C7, D5, I2
What number plus 90 was the age of Abraham when he was circumcised? (Genesis 17:24)

For A8, B6, F7, H9
On what day of creation were plants and trees made by God? (Genesis 1:11–13)

For C3, E6, G9
How many helpers did Paul send to Macedonia while he stayed in Asia a little longer? (Acts 19:21–22)

For A3, C9, D2, I6
How many months did Zachariah reign in Israel? (2 Kings 15:8)

For E1, F8, G5, I3
In God's promised blessings for the Israelites' obedience, how many people would chase a hundred enemies? (Leviticus 26:3, 8)

For A5, E3, F4
How many children did Absalom have? (2 Samuel 14:27)

For E7, H5
How many days did the prophet Ezekiel sit with captives at Tel-abib near the river? (Ezekiel 3:15)

For C4, D7, F2, I1
What number plus 4 equals the "basket full of the fragments" left over from the feeding of the five thousand? (Mark 6:42)

For I8
How many servants escaped the Chaldeans' raiding bands to tell Job? (Job 1:17)

	A	B	C	D	E	F	G	H	I
1									
2									
3									
4									
5									
6									
7									
8									
9									

Starter Numbers in Order:
6, 3, 2, 9, 5, 4, 7, 8, 1

PUZZLE 77

	A	B	C	D	E	F	G	H	I
1	H	O	N				K	A	E
2			E		O	N			H
3			T				R		N
4	O	R	G		T		A		
5	E	H					N		
6	T	N	K		A		G		
7					G		O		
8	N				H			T	A
9		E	R			T	H	K	G

Hint: Row 3

Two of the five Philistine capital cities under God's judgment were _____ and _____. (1 Samuel 5:8–10)

PUZZLE 78

	A	B	C	D	E	F	G	H	I
1			E				L	N	
2	O							U	R
3			R		B		I		E
4						N			
5			L		R				
6		U	N	T	I		R	B	O
7		B	T						U
8	R					O	E		
9	I					T	B	L	N

Hint: Column B

David begged God not to hide Himself when David was __ ________. (Psalm 69:17)

PUZZLE 79

For A4, E5
What number plus 111 was the number of princes set over the kingdom by Darius? (Daniel 6:1)

For C3, E4, H9
In a scene in Revelation, how many of God's dead prophets will earth's inhabitants rejoice over? (Revelation 11:9–10)

For C4, D1, E6
Of the four faces in Ezekiel's vision, how many were of a lion? (Ezekiel 10:14)

For A2, B6, D7, E1
In a question posed by some Sadducees to Jesus, how many of seven brothers died without leaving children? (Mark 12:18, 22)

For E7, F3, I4
How many cities of refuge did God tell Moses to institute? (Numbers 35:15)

For G1
What number times 5 was the number of days Jesus stayed on earth after His resurrection? (Acts 1:3)

For C7, F5, G3, I9
When twelve-year-old Jesus was separated from His parents in Jerusalem, how many days passed before they found Him in the temple? (Luke 2:41–46)

For C8, D9, G4
How old was Jonathan's son Mephibosheth when he became lame? (2 Samuel 4:4)

For B8, C2, G7, H4, I1
When David made Solomon king, how many thousand praised the Lord with musical instruments? (1 Chronicles 23:1, 5)

	A	B	C	D	E	F	G	H	I
1									
2									
3									
4									
5									
6									
7									
8									
9									

Starter Numbers in Order:
9, 2, 1, 7, 6, 8, 3, 5, 4

PUZZLE 80

For C1, E4, I5
How many of Saul's sons died in battle with him? (1 Samuel 31:8)

For A6, E9, H7
How many wives did Elkanah have? (1 Samuel 1:1–2)

For G9, H1, I4
Of the first nine psalms, which one begins, "I will praise thee, O LORD, with my whole heart"?

For D9
How many months was Shallum king of Israel? (2 Kings 15:13)

For C5, E6, F3, H9
Of the first nine psalms, which psalm says in verse 2, "Out of the mouth of babes"?

For A8, D2, I3
How many golden mice were sent to Israel as part of a tresspass offering from the Philistines, along with the ark of the Lord? (1 Samuel 6:1, 4)

For A7, B2, E3
How many eunuchs (or chamberlains) served King Ahasuerus? (Esther 1:10)

For A4, F1, H2
What number times 10 was the age of Moses when he smote an Egyptian for mistreating an Israelite? (Acts 7:22–24)

For D7, E2, I8
Of the first nine chapters of Isaiah, which chapter begins, "In the year that king Uzziah died I saw also the Lord"?

	A	B	C	D	E	F	G	H	I
1									
2									
3									
4									
5									
6									
7									
8									
9									

Starter Numbers in Order:
3, 2, 9, 1, 8, 5, 7, 4, 6

PUZZLE 81

For E2, H8
How many sons did Benjamin have? (1 Chronicles 7:6)

For A3, H2
How many days did Samson give the young men to answer his riddle? (Judges 14:12)

For C7, E5, F1, I6
What number plus 1,000 was the number of songs accredited to Solomon? (1 Kings 4:29, 32)

For D8, I5
How many Old Testament figures appeared at Jesus' transfiguration? (Matthew 17:1–3)

For E6, I8
How many quaternions of soldiers were ordered to guard Peter after King Herod arrested him? (Acts 12:1–4)

For C4, G6, I1
How many working days were ordained by God? (Exodus 20:9)

For C1, E9, F5
How many beatitudes are listed in Matthew 5:3–11?

For A6, G2
According to Peter, how many souls were on Noah's ark? (1 Peter 3:20)

For A8, B1, D4, H7
On what day of the tenth month after the flood did the mountains become visible? (Genesis 8:5)

	A	B	C	D	E	F	G	H	I
1									
2									
3									
4									
5									
6									
7									
8									
9									

Starter Numbers in Order:
3, 7, 5, 2, 4, 6, 9, 8, 1

PUZZLE 82

	A	B	C	D	E	F	G	H	I
1	I								D
2					C		O		
3			E	F	R				
4						R		I	
5	E			D			C		
6		F	L				E		
7					E				
8			D			I	F		
9			O	U				R	

Hint: Row 9

God led the Israelites in the wilderness by a pillar of _____ by day and of ____ by night. (Exodus 13:21)

PUZZLE 83

	A	B	C	D	E	F	G	H	I
1									Y
2	K	S		Y		O		T	E
3	Y	N							D
4	E	A	Y		D		K		N
5	S		N	E				D	A
6		O	K						T
7	A	D				T	E		
8	N		O					A	K
9			E		Y		D		

Hint: Column E

Jesus ___ on a _______ while people threw down palm leaves before Him. (John 12:13–14 NIV)

PUZZLE 84

	A	B	C	D	E	F	G	H	I
1		O		E	R	T			N
2	R		T					E	
3	N		A			W	R	O	T
4								L	H
5						A			
6	E	W	R			L	O		A
7	H	R			W	O			
8		N							O
9	W	T	O	N	L			H	R

Hint: Row 1

God made men to be a little _____ ____ the angels.
(Psalm 8:5)

PUZZLE 85

	A	B	C	D	E	F	G	H	I
1				N			O	B	
2		B			I	T			
3		T	S				M		
4		E		I		S	R		
5		O					E	S	
6	R				E	M			
7		N		E					
8	B	M		S				N	R
9					M			E	

Hint: Column H

God made fire and __________ rain down on Sodom and Gomorrah. (Genesis 19:24)

PUZZLE 86

	A	B	C	D	E	F	G	H	I
1					K			N	
2	N	R	K		S				
3			A			R			E
4		B	N	O	W		E		K
5		K		R	B	A		S	
6								B	
7			S	B			K	E	
8			O		N			W	A
9				W				O	R

Hint: Row 7

Part of Paul's shipwrecked boat included the stern (hinder part) that ___ _______ from stormy waves. (Acts 27:41)

PUZZLE 87

	A	B	C	D	E	F	G	H	I
1	I	N			S	E	H		T
2					R		S		
3			P	T		H	R		
4	H							T	O
5		E			H		P		R
6	O	P	S			N	I		
7			H		E				
8	P	I		S	O	T	E		
9			O		I	R		N	P

Hint: Row 2

An angel of the Lord opened ___ _______ doors.
(Acts 5:19)

PUZZLE 88

For A3, E4, G5
For many deceivers are entered into the world, who confess not that Jesus Christ is come in the flesh. This is a deceiver and an antichrist. (2 John 1:_)

For A7, B2, D9, E6, F1, H5
Set your affection on things above, not on things on the earth. (Colossians 3:_)

For B1, E5, G6
And the second angel sounded, and as it were a great mountain burning with fire was cast into the sea: and the third part of the sea became blood. (Revelation 8:_)

For B4, C8, D1, F5, I3
Yet for love's sake I rather beseech thee, being such an one as Paul the aged, and now also a prisoner of Jesus Christ. (Philemon _)

For B5, D7, E2, H9
But now hath he obtained a more excellent ministry, by how much also he is the mediator of a better covenant, which was established upon better promises. (Hebrews 8:_)

For B8, C2, D3, H1
Christ is become of no effect unto you, whosoever of you are justified by the law; ye are fallen from grace. (Galatians 5:_)

For B9, C6, D5, E8, F3, H2, I7
Then Jerubbaal, who is Gideon, and all the people that were with him, rose up early, and pitched beside the well of Harod. (Judges 7:_)

For C5, F7, G2, H8
And the second angel poured out his vial upon the sea; and it became as the blood of a dead man: and every living soul died in the sea. (Revelation 16:_)

For F9, G8, H4
Having a form of godliness, but denying the power thereof: from such turn away. (2 Timothy 3:_)

	A	B	C	D	E	F	G	H	I
1									
2									
3									
4									
5									
6									
7									
8									
9									

Starter Numbers in Order:
7, 2, 8, 9, 6, 4, 1, 3, 5

PUZZLE 89

For A1, C7, D3, E8, F6, H2, I5
So king Solomon was king over all Israel. (1 Kings 4:_)

For A3, D2, G4, H8, I1
And when the queen of Sheba had seen all Solomon's wisdom, and the house that he had built. . . (1 Kings 10:_)

For A4, B1, D6, H5, I7
The Lord knoweth how to deliver the godly out of temptations, and to reserve the unjust unto the day of judgment to be punished. (2 Peter 2:_)

For A5, C3, D4, F9
Who then is Paul, and who is Apollos, but ministers by whom ye believed, even as the Lord gave to every man? (1 Corinthians 3:_)

For A7, C6, D8, E5, F2, H9
Even as the testimony of Christ was confirmed in you. . . (1 Corinthians 1:_)

For A9, B5, D1, F8, G3, I6
But we were gentle among you, even as a nurse cherisheth her children. (1 Thessalonians 2:_)

For B2, F1, G7, I3
And having food and raiment let us be therewith content. (1 Timothy 6:_)

For B8, C4, F7, G6, H1, I9
And be not conformed to this world: but be ye transformed by the renewing of your mind, that ye may prove what is that good, and acceptable, and perfect, will of God. (Romans 12:_)

For B9, E2, F4
And not only so, but we glory in tribulations also: knowing that tribulation worketh patience. (Romans 5:_)

	A	B	C	D	E	F	G	H	I
1									
2									
3									
4									
5									
6									
7									
8									
9									

Starter Numbers in Order:
1, 4, 9, 5, 6, 7, 8, 2, 3

PUZZLE 90

For A1, C5, H3
For I am jealous over you with godly jealousy: for I have espoused you to one husband, that I may present you as a chaste virgin to Christ. (2 Corinthians 11:_)

For A3, B5, D8, E6
And they sing the song of Moses the servant of God, and the song of the Lamb, saying, Great and marvellous are thy works, Lord God Almighty. (Revelation 15:_)

For A6, F5, G2, H4, I7
Insomuch that we desired Titus, that as he had begun, so he would also finish in you the same grace also. (2 Corinthians 8:_)

For A7, C3, F2, G8, I5
And it came to pass, when they were gone over, that Elijah said unto Elisha, Ask what I shall do for thee, before I be taken away from thee. And Elisha said, I pray thee, let a double portion of thy spirit be upon me. (2 Kings 2:_)

For A9, F7, G1, H8
For God hath not given us the spirit of fear; but of power, and of love, and of a sound mind. (2 Timothy 1:_)

For B1, C6, D2, E4, F9, H5, I3
In the beginning God created the heaven and the earth. (Genesis 1:_)

For B4, C8, D9, G5, H7, I1
For it came to pass, when Solomon was old, that his wives turned away his heart after other gods: and his heart was not perfect with the LORD his God, as was the heart of David his father. (1 Kings 11:_)

For B7, D5, E1, H6, I9
Remember that Jesus Christ of the seed of David was raised from the dead according to my gospel. (2 Timothy 2:_)

For B8, C1, F3
For as the sufferings of Christ abound in us, so our consolation also aboundeth by Christ. (2 Corinthians 1:_)

	A	B	C	D	E	F	G	H	I
1									
2									
3									
4									
5									
6									
7									
8									
9									

Starter Numbers in Order:
2, 3, 6, 9, 7, 1, 4, 8, 5

PUZZLE 91

	A	B	C	D	E	F	G	H	I
1	H			F	W		T		R
2	O	T		A		H		F	V
3		R			I	T			
4			T		H		A	V	
5	V	O	F			A		W	I
6	I			W	F	V			T
7	T	H			V	W			A
8			O		A	F		I	H
9	A			H		R	V	T	

Hint: Column D

And the boy Samuel continued to grow in stature and in ______ ______ the LORD and with men. (1 Samuel 2:26 NIV)

PUZZLE 92

	A	B	C	D	E	F	G	H	I
1	S	O		E	T			N	G
2	I		T	G				O	
3		N			M	I	S		E
4	E		N		O			H	
5		G			S		E		O
6		T		H		G		M	
7	N			S		E			I
8	T				G				N
9		H	E	N	I		O	S	

Hint: Row 1

Jesus replied, "They do not need to go away. You give them __________ to eat." (Matthew 14:16 NIV)

PUZZLE 93

For A1, B7, D3, G2
And it shall be, that thou shalt drink of the brook; and I have commanded the ravens to feed thee there. (1 Kings 17:_)

For A3, C9, D5, F1, G4, H2, I7
And cast him into the bottomless pit, and shut him up, and set a seal upon him, that he should deceive the nations no more, till the thousand years should be fulfilled. (Revelation 20:_)

For A4, D8, F3, G6, I9
Then sang Deborah and Barak the son of Abinoam on that day, saying. . . (Judges 5:_)

For A5, B8, E7, F2, G1, H9, I6
Honour thy father and mother; which is the first commandment with promise. (Ephesians 6:_)

For A8, C1, D9
Circumcised the eighth day, of the stock of Israel, of the tribe of Benjamin, an Hebrew of the Hebrews; as touching the law, a Pharisee. . . (Philippians 3:_)

For B1, C8, E4, F7, G9, H3, I5
Now as Jannes and Jambres withstood Moses, so do these also resist the truth: men of corrupt minds, reprobate concerning the faith. (2 Timothy 3:_)

For C2, E6, H8
For in Jesus Christ neither circumcision availeth any thing, nor uncircumcision; but faith which worketh by love. (Galatians 5:_)

For C4, E3, G7, H5
I have fought a good fight, I have finished my course, I have kept the faith. (2 Timothy 4:_)

For C6, D7, F5, I2
If we confess our sins, he is faithful and just to forgive us our sins, and to cleanse us from all unrighteousness. (1 John 1:_)

	A	B	C	D	E	F	G	H	I
1									
2									
3									
4									
5									
6									
7									
8									
9									

Starter Numbers in Order:
4, 3, 1, 2, 5, 8, 6, 7, 9

PUZZLE 94

For A1, B6, C8
In this was manifested the love of God toward us, because that God sent his only begotten Son into the world, that we might live through him. (1 John 4:_)

For A3, C7, D4, F9, G6, I8
Henceforth there is laid up for me a crown of righteousness, which the Lord, the righteous judge, shall give me at that day. (2 Timothy 4:_)

For A6, C3, D2, G1, H8
And after Abimelech there arose to defend Israel Tola the son of Puah. (Judges 10:_)

For A7, C1, D3, E6, F8
He that keepeth his mouth keepeth his life: but he that openeth wide his lips shall have destruction. (Proverbs 13:_)

For A9, E8, F1, G3, H4, I7
So that ye were ensamples to all that believe in Macedonia and Achaia. . . (1 Thessalonians 1:_)

For B9, C6, F7
And because ye are sons, God hath sent forth the Spirit of his Son into your hearts, crying, Abba, Father. (Galatians 4:_)

For C2, D9, E5, I1
And it came to pass, afore Isaiah was gone out into the middle court, that the word of the LORD came to him saying. . . (2 Kings 20:_)

For C4, E1, G9, H5, I2
Your riches are corrupted, and your garments are motheaten. (James 5:_)

For F4, H7, I6
And the Lord direct your hearts into the love of God, and into the patient waiting for Christ. (2 Thessalonians 3:_)

	A	B	C	D	E	F	G	H	I
1									
2									
3									
4									
5									
6									
7									
8									
9									

Starter Numbers in Order:
6, 8, 1, 3, 7, 9, 4, 2, 5

PUZZLE 95

For A1, E7, I4
Sound speech, that cannot be condemned; that he that is of the contrary part may be ashamed, having no evil thing to say of you. . . (Titus 2:_)

For A3, B4, H5
And the children of Israel again did evil in the sight of the LORD, when Ehud was dead. (Judges 4:_)

For A5, B1, C9, D6, F3, G4, I7
The eyes of the LORD are in every place, beholding the evil and the good. (Proverbs 15:_)

For A8, F1, I3
In all things shewing thyself a pattern of good works: in doctrine shewing uncorruptness, gravity, sincerity. . . (Titus 2:_)

For A9, B6, E5, F8
Being confident of this very thing, that he which hath begun a good work in you will perform it until the day of Jesus Christ. (Philippians 1:_)

For B5, C3, E2, F9, G8, H1, I6
As newborn babes, desire the sincere milk of the word, that ye may grow thereby. (1 Peter 2:_)

For B7, C5, D1, F4, G3
But he that lacketh these things is blind, and cannot see afar off, and hath forgotten that he was purged from his old sins. (2 Peter 1:_)

For D8, F2, H9
And let the maiden which pleaseth the king be queen instead of Vashti. And the thing pleased the king; and he did so. (Esther 2:_)

For G6, H8, I2
For there is one God, and one mediator between God and men, the man Christ Jesus. (1 Timothy 2:_)

	A	B	C	D	E	F	G	H	I
1									
2									
3									
4									
5									
6									
7									
8									
9									

Starter Numbers in Order:
8, 1, 3, 7, 6, 2, 9, 4, 5

PUZZLE 96

	A	B	C	D	E	F	G	H	I
1		H		M	I	S		T	O
2	E		T		H				
3	O		S	E			I		L
4	I				L			E	
5	F			S			L		H
6		L	H	I	E		S		M
7	H		L	T	O	E		S	
8		T	I	F			O		
9	S		E			I	H	F	

Hint: Column B

The victim commits ________ __ you. (Psalm 10:14 NIV)

PUZZLE 97

	A	B	C	D	E	F	G	H	I
1		C		E	N	R	L	S	
2			N		L	C			R
3	L	R		U			E		N
4	C			N			I	U	
5	S	I	L		C				E
6		U		R	I			L	
7	R			L		I		E	
8	U		O		R	N	C		
9		L			U	E		N	O

Hint: Row 4

And they said, __________ the centurion, a just man, and one that feareth God. . . (Acts 10:22)

PUZZLE 98

For A2, B6, C8, D7, G9, I3
But unto the Son he saith, Thy throne, O God, is for ever and ever: a sceptre of righteousness is the scepter of thy kingdom. (Hebrews 1:_)

For A3, B7, C5, E8, I4
And they continued three years without war between Syria and Israel. (1 Kings 22:_)

For A6, D1, H4
For it is sanctified by the word of God and prayer. (1 Timothy 4:_)

For A7, E3, F5, H2
Hereby know ye the Spirit of God: Every spirit that confesseth that Jesus Christ is come in the flesh is of God. (1 John 4:_)

For B8, D9, E4, F3, G6, H7, I1
Then the king held out the golden sceptre toward Esther. So Esther arose, and stood before the king. (Esther 8:_)

For C1, E7, H3
Yet Michael the archangel, when contending with the devil he disputed about the body of Moses, durst not bring against him a railing accusation, but said, The Lord rebuke thee. (Jude _)

For C4, D3, E6, F7, G5, I8
Be careful for nothing; but in every thing by prayer and supplication with thanksgiving let your requests be made known unto God. (Philippians 4:_)

For D5, E2, F9
A prudent man foreseeth the evil, and hideth himself: but the simple pass on, and are punished. (Proverbs 22:_)

For F1, G2, I7
And the peace of God, which passeth all understanding, shall keep your hearts and minds through Christ Jesus. (Philippians 4:_)

	A	B	C	D	E	F	G	H	I
1									
2									
3									
4									
5									
6									
7									
8									
9									

Starter Numbers in Order:
8, 1, 5, 2, 4, 9, 6, 3, 7

PUZZLE 99

For A1, B7
For God hath not called us unto uncleanness, but unto holiness. (1 Thessalonians 4:_)

For A3, D1, F4, I2
Let your speech be always with grace, seasoned with salt, that ye may know how ye ought to answer every man. (Colossians 4:_)

For A6, D9, F2, I5
I John, who also am your brother, and companion in tribulation, and in the kingdom and patience of Jesus Christ, was in the isle that is called Patmos, for the word of God, and for the testimony of Jesus Christ. (Revelation 1:_)

For A8, C6, D7, E2, F5, G4, H3
While they behold your chaste conversation coupled with fear. . . (1 Peter 3:_)

For A9, B4, D3, E5, G8, H2
For Mordecai was great in the king's house, and his fame went out throughout all the provinces: for this man Mordecai waxed greater and greater. (Esther 9:_)

For B2, D5, G1, H6
But if ye be without chastisement, whereof all are partakers, then are ye bastards, and not sons. (Hebrews 12:_)

For B3, C9, D6, E8, F1, I7
Now the end of the commandment is charity out of a pure heart, and of a good conscience, and of faith unfeigned. (1 Timothy 1:_)

For C2, F3, G5, H8, I1
Josiah was eight years old when he began to reign, and he reigned thirty and one years in Jerusalem. (2 Kings 22:_)

For C5, D8, H7, I4
Through wisdom is an house builded; and by understanding it is established. (Proverbs 24:_)

	A	B	C	D	E	F	G	H	I
1									
2									
3									
4									
5									
6									
7									
8									
9									

Starter Numbers in Order:
7, 6, 9, 2, 4, 8, 5, 1, 3

PUZZLE 100

For A2, C7, E8, F1, G5, H3, I9
For if that first covenant had been faultless, then should no place have been sought for the second. (Hebrews 8:_)

For A3, B6, C9, D5, G8, H1
And it was told Saul that David was fled to Gath: and he sought no more again for him. (1 Samuel 27:_)

For A5, B7, D8, E3, G2, I6
Therefore let us not sleep, as do others; but let us watch and be sober. (1 Thessalonians 5:_)

For A9, C6, D1, F8, I7
Now when Ezra had prayed, and when he had confessed, weeping and casting himself down before the house of God. . . (Ezra 10:_)

For B1, D2, F6
To know wisdom and instruction; to perceive the words of understanding. . . (Proverbs 1:_)

For B2, C5, G7, H4, I1
A poor man that oppresseth the poor is like a sweeping rain which leaveth no food. (Proverbs 28:_)

For B8, E4, F9, I5
And when he had opened the fifth seal, I saw under the altar the souls of them that were slain for the word of God, and for the testimony which they held. (Revelation 6:_)

For C3, F5, H8, I2
Not by works of righteousness which we have done, but according to his mercy he saved us, by the washing of regeneration, and renewing of the Holy Ghost. (Titus 3:_)

For E7, H6
Though he were a Son, yet learned he obedience by the things which he suffered. (Hebrews 5:_)

	A	B	C	D	E	F	G	H	I
1									
2									
3									
4									
5									
6									
7									
8									
9									

Starter Numbers in Order:
7, 4, 6, 1, 2, 3, 9, 5, 8

PUZZLE 101

For A3, B5, C8, D1, E4
Thou madest him a little lower than the angels; thou crownedst him with glory and honour, and didst set him over the works of thy hands. (Hebrews 2:_)

For A4, E9, F6, G7
Keep my commandments, and live; and my law as the apple of thine eye. (Proverbs 7:_)

For A7, B1, F8, G5, H9, I2
Who gave himself a ransom for all, to be testified in due time. . . (1 Timothy 2:_)

For B3, E2, I7
And they sung a new song, saying, Thou art worthy to take the book, and to open the seals thereof: for thou was slain, and hast redeemed us to God by thy blood. (Revelation 5:_)

For B4, D5, F2, G9
And he said unto him, Why art thou, being the king's son, lean from day to day? wilt thou not tell me? And Amnon said unto him, I love Tamar, my brother Absalom's sister. (2 Samuel 13:_)

For B7, D9, F5, I6
On that night could not the king sleep, and he commanded to bring the book of records of the chronicles; and they were read before the king. (Esther 6:_)

For B9, E6, F3, G2, I4
Let your conversation be without covetousness; and be content with such things as ye have: for he hath said, I will never leave thee, nor forsake thee. (Hebrews 13:_)

For C2, D7, F1, G4, H3, I8
Every moving thing that liveth shall be meat for you; even as the green herb have I given you all things. (Genesis 9:_)

For C9, E7, H1
Be not thou therefore ashamed of the testimony of our Lord, nor of me his prisoner: but be thou partaker of the afflictions of the gospel according to the power of God. (2 Timothy 1:_)

	A	B	C	D	E	F	G	H	I
1									
2									
3									
4									
5									
6									
7									
8									
9									

Starter Numbers in Order:
7, 2, 6, 9, 4, 1, 5, 3, 8

PUZZLE 102

	A	B	C	D	E	F	G	H	I
1			N			E	H	O	R
2	M	O		H	N				
3			H		I		M	B	
4	H				R	N	B		I
5	N	E		B					
6		Z	R		M			N	E
7	O	H	Z	R			N	I	
8	R				O	I	Z		
9			M			B			O

Hint: Column G

But the Philistines took him. . .and bound ___ with fetters of _______/brass; and he did grind in the prison house. (Judges 16:21)

PUZZLE 103

	A	B	C	D	E	F	G	H	I
1				I		N	S		D
2	I	H	G			S		L	
3	N	D		H		K	G		
4		S			N				H
5		N		K			I		
6	G	K		S	I		O		L
7		O	L					G	K
8			N	G	H	O		D	S
9	S					D			O

Hint: Row 8

They put him in ward in chains, and brought him to the ____ of Babylon: they brought him into _____, that his voice should no more be heard upon the mountains of Israel. (Ezekiel 19:9)

PUZZLE 104

For A1, B6, C9, D4, G8, H3, I5
A double minded man is unstable in all his ways. (James 1:_)

For A2, C7, F6
And when the woman of Tekoah spake to the king, she fell on her face to the ground, and did obeisance, and said, Help, O king. (2 Samuel 14:_)

For A4, D6, E3, F9, G5
Now Benjamin begat Bela his firstborn, Ashbel the second, and Aharah the third. (1 Chronicles 8:_)

For A6, D7, G2, I4
A wise servant shall have rule over a son that causeth shame, and shall have part of the inheritance among the brethren. (Proverbs 17:_)

For A7, C6, D5, E8, F2
But let him ask in faith, nothing wavering. For he that wavereth is like a wave of the sea driven with the wind and tossed. (James 1:_)

For A8, B5, C2, F1, I7
That being justified by his grace, we should be made heirs according to the hope of eternal life. (Titus 3:_)

For B1, C4, F5, G6
If any of you lack wisdom, let him ask of God, that giveth to all men liberally, and upbraideth not; and it shall be given him. (James 1:_)

For C3, D2, F4, G7, H1, I6
And I went unto the angel, and said unto him, Give me the little book. And he said unto me, Take it, and eat it up; and it shall make thy belly bitter, but it shall be in thy mouth sweet as honey. (Revelation 10:_)

For D1, G4, H9, I2
And Sarai Abram's wife took Hagar her maid the Egyptian, after Abram had dwelt ten years in the land of Canaan, and gave her to her husband Abram to be his wife. (Genesis 16:_)

	A	B	C	D	E	F	G	H	I
1									
2									
3									
4									
5									
6									
7									
8									
9									

Starter Numbers in Order:
8, 4, 1, 2, 6, 7, 5, 9, 3

ANSWERS

I	H	E	L	S	T	M	O	A
A	T	M	I	O	H	S	L	E
O	S	L	M	E	A	T	H	I
L	A	H	T	I	E	O	S	M
E	M	S	A	L	O	I	T	H
T	O	I	S	H	M	A	E	L
M	E	T	H	A	S	L	I	O
H	L	A	O	T	I	E	M	S
S	I	O	E	M	L	H	A	T

PUZZLE 1

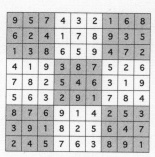

9	5	7	4	3	2	1	6	8
6	2	4	1	7	8	9	3	5
1	3	8	6	5	9	4	7	2
4	1	9	3	8	7	5	2	6
7	8	2	5	4	6	3	1	9
5	6	3	2	9	1	7	8	4
8	7	6	9	1	4	2	5	3
3	9	1	8	2	5	6	4	7
2	4	5	7	6	3	8	9	1

PUZZLE 2

7	5	6	3	1	8	4	9	2
2	4	3	6	7	9	1	5	8
9	1	8	4	5	2	3	6	7
5	3	2	9	6	4	8	7	1
6	8	1	2	3	7	5	4	9
4	7	9	5	8	1	2	3	6
3	2	7	1	4	6	9	8	5
1	6	4	8	9	5	7	2	3
8	9	5	7	2	3	6	1	4

PUZZLE 3

8	4	3	1	5	7	9	2	6
5	9	7	4	2	6	3	8	1
6	1	2	9	3	8	7	5	4
9	6	1	3	7	2	8	4	5
3	8	5	6	4	1	2	7	9
2	7	4	5	8	9	1	6	3
1	5	8	2	6	3	4	9	7
7	3	6	8	9	4	5	1	2
4	2	9	7	1	5	6	3	8

PUZZLE 4

1	4	5	6	2	9	7	3	8
9	6	2	8	3	7	1	4	5
7	8	3	5	1	4	9	6	2
8	5	1	2	7	3	4	9	6
6	9	4	1	5	8	2	7	3
2	3	7	4	9	6	5	8	1
3	2	6	7	4	5	8	1	9
4	1	9	3	8	2	6	5	7
5	7	8	9	6	1	3	2	4

PUZZLE 5

6	7	2	1	8	3	4	5	9
4	1	3	6	5	9	7	2	8
9	5	8	7	4	2	1	3	6
5	9	6	2	1	4	8	7	3
2	8	4	5	3	7	9	6	1
1	3	7	9	6	8	2	4	5
8	4	5	3	7	1	6	9	2
7	6	9	8	2	5	3	1	4
3	2	1	4	9	6	5	8	7

PUZZLE 6

9	7	6	2	4	8	3	1	5
8	4	3	1	6	5	7	2	9
1	5	2	7	9	3	4	6	8
6	1	7	5	3	4	8	9	2
2	8	5	6	7	9	1	3	4
4	3	9	8	2	1	6	5	7
7	2	8	3	5	6	9	4	1
3	9	1	4	8	2	5	7	6
5	6	4	9	1	7	2	8	3

PUZZLE 7

7	5	6	3	1	8	4	9	2
2	4	3	6	7	9	1	5	8
9	1	8	4	5	2	3	6	7
5	3	2	9	6	4	8	7	1
6	8	1	2	3	7	5	4	9
4	7	9	5	8	1	2	3	6
3	2	7	1	4	6	9	8	5
1	6	4	8	9	5	7	2	3
8	9	5	7	2	3	6	1	4

PUZZLE 8

6	1	9	5	4	8	3	7	2
8	3	5	9	2	7	4	1	6
7	4	2	3	6	1	8	9	5
9	2	3	1	5	4	6	8	7
4	8	6	2	7	3	9	5	1
1	5	7	8	9	6	2	3	4
3	7	4	6	1	9	5	2	8
2	6	8	7	3	5	1	4	9
5	9	1	4	8	2	7	6	3

PUZZLE 9

H	K	I	Y	O	M	E	N	L
O	M	L	N	E	I	Y	K	H
E	Y	N	H	K	L	I	M	O
L	N	H	M	Y	K	O	E	I
K	I	O	E	N	H	M	L	Y
M	E	Y	I	L	O	K	H	N
Y	O	E	K	H	N	L	I	M
N	L	M	O	I	E	H	Y	K
I	H	K	L	M	Y	N	O	E

PUZZLE 10

G	A	S	I	F	N	R	K	O
K	I	R	G	O	A	S	N	F
F	O	N	K	R	S	I	A	G
A	K	F	N	S	R	O	G	I
R	N	G	O	A	I	F	S	K
I	S	O	F	K	G	N	R	A
N	G	K	R	I	O	A	F	S
S	F	I	A	N	K	G	O	R
O	R	A	S	G	F	K	I	N

PUZZLE 11

3	1	9	4	8	6	2	7	5
7	2	4	1	9	5	8	6	3
8	5	6	7	3	2	1	9	4
9	3	1	8	4	7	5	2	6
6	4	5	3	2	1	7	8	9
2	8	7	6	5	9	4	3	1
1	6	2	5	7	3	9	4	8
5	9	8	2	6	4	3	1	7
4	7	3	9	1	8	6	5	2

PUZZLE 12

2	5	3	7	6	8	1	9	4
4	9	6	3	2	1	5	8	7
8	7	1	9	4	5	6	2	3
7	4	2	8	3	6	9	1	5
6	1	9	5	7	2	3	4	8
3	8	5	1	9	4	7	6	2
5	2	4	6	1	3	8	7	9
9	6	8	4	5	7	2	3	1
1	3	7	2	8	9	4	5	6

PUZZLE 13

9	5	7	2	8	4	6	3	1
1	2	8	9	3	6	5	4	7
3	6	4	7	5	1	9	8	2
8	1	6	5	9	7	4	2	3
2	9	3	6	4	8	1	7	5
4	7	5	3	1	2	8	9	6
7	8	2	4	6	5	3	1	9
5	4	9	1	2	3	7	6	8
6	3	1	8	7	9	2	5	4

PUZZLE 14

1	8	6	4	3	2	7	5	9
4	3	2	9	7	5	6	1	8
7	9	5	6	8	1	2	4	3
5	2	4	1	9	3	8	6	7
9	7	8	2	4	6	1	3	5
6	1	3	8	5	7	4	9	2
3	4	1	7	2	9	5	8	6
8	5	7	3	6	4	9	2	1
2	6	9	5	1	8	3	7	4

PUZZLE 15

5	2	8	3	9	1	4	7	6
7	1	3	2	4	6	8	5	9
9	4	6	7	5	8	2	1	3
2	3	7	4	6	5	1	9	8
4	5	1	8	3	9	7	6	2
8	6	9	1	7	2	3	4	5
1	9	4	6	2	3	5	8	7
6	7	2	5	8	4	9	3	1
3	8	5	9	1	7	6	2	4

PUZZLE 16

5	1	9	8	7	4	6	2	3
3	8	4	1	6	2	9	7	5
2	7	6	5	9	3	4	1	8
6	4	2	3	8	9	1	5	7
8	9	5	7	4	1	3	6	2
7	3	1	2	5	6	8	9	4
1	5	8	9	3	7	2	4	6
9	6	3	4	2	5	7	8	1
4	2	7	6	1	8	5	3	9

PUZZLE 17

5	1	3	4	6	2	7	9	8
4	6	7	3	8	9	1	2	5
8	9	2	5	7	1	6	3	4
6	3	9	2	5	4	8	7	1
7	4	5	9	1	8	3	6	2
2	8	1	7	3	6	5	4	9
3	2	8	1	9	7	4	5	6
1	5	4	6	2	3	9	8	7
9	7	6	8	4	5	2	1	3

PUZZLE 18

3	8	7	6	2	5	4	9	1
4	2	6	8	1	9	7	3	5
5	1	9	7	3	4	2	6	8
2	4	1	9	8	6	5	7	3
6	3	5	2	7	1	8	4	9
9	7	8	4	5	3	6	1	2
8	6	3	1	4	2	9	5	7
1	9	2	5	6	7	3	8	4
7	5	4	3	9	8	1	2	6

PUZZLE 19

E	S	P	D	G	O	R	A	I
D	I	R	P	S	A	O	G	E
G	O	A	I	R	E	S	D	P
A	R	I	S	D	P	G	E	O
O	G	S	E	A	R	I	P	D
P	D	E	O	I	G	A	S	R
S	E	G	R	P	I	D	O	A
R	A	O	G	E	D	P	I	S
I	P	D	A	O	S	E	R	G

PUZZLE 20

H	T	I	O	N	G	M	E	Y
O	G	N	Y	E	M	I	T	H
Y	E	M	I	T	H	G	O	N
G	N	T	E	I	Y	H	M	O
E	Y	H	N	M	O	T	I	G
M	I	O	H	G	T	Y	N	E
N	M	E	G	Y	I	O	H	T
I	O	G	T	H	E	N	Y	M
T	H	Y	M	O	N	E	G	I

PUZZLE 21

7	5	3	4	6	2	8	9	1
4	1	8	7	3	9	5	2	6
6	2	9	8	1	5	7	3	4
8	6	2	9	4	1	3	7	5
5	3	1	6	2	7	9	4	8
9	4	7	3	5	8	1	6	2
1	8	6	2	9	3	4	5	7
3	7	4	5	8	6	2	1	9
2	9	5	1	7	4	6	8	3

PUZZLE 22

6	1	8	3	7	5	2	9	4
5	7	2	9	4	1	3	6	8
9	3	4	8	6	2	1	7	5
3	4	7	1	9	8	6	5	2
1	6	5	2	3	4	9	8	7
8	2	9	6	5	7	4	3	1
7	8	6	4	2	3	5	1	9
2	9	1	5	8	6	7	4	3
4	5	3	7	1	9	8	2	6

PUZZLE 23

1	4	2	8	3	7	5	9	6
7	3	9	1	5	6	2	4	8
8	6	5	4	2	9	7	1	3
6	1	4	3	8	2	9	7	5
5	7	3	6	9	1	8	2	4
9	2	8	5	7	4	6	3	1
2	8	1	9	4	5	3	6	7
3	9	6	7	1	8	4	5	2
4	5	7	2	6	3	1	8	9

PUZZLE 24

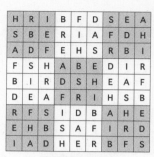

2	7	1	5	4	3	9	8	6
6	5	8	1	2	9	3	4	7
9	3	4	6	7	8	1	2	5
1	6	5	2	8	7	4	9	3
7	9	2	3	5	4	6	1	8
8	4	3	9	6	1	7	5	2
4	1	7	8	3	5	2	6	9
3	8	6	4	9	2	5	7	1
5	2	9	7	1	6	8	3	4

PUZZLE 25

H	R	I	B	F	D	S	E	A
S	B	E	R	I	A	F	D	H
A	D	F	E	H	S	R	B	I
F	S	H	A	B	E	D	I	R
B	I	R	D	S	H	E	A	F
D	E	A	F	R	I	H	S	B
R	F	S	I	D	B	A	H	E
E	H	B	S	A	F	I	R	D
I	A	D	H	E	R	B	F	S

PUZZLE 26

T	R	H	S	O	N	I	B	E
I	S	E	R	B	T	H	O	N
B	O	N	E	H	I	S	R	T
S	T	I	H	R	E	B	N	O
O	E	R	B	N	S	T	I	H
H	N	B	I	T	O	E	S	R
N	I	S	O	E	H	R	T	B
E	B	O	T	S	R	N	H	I
R	H	T	N	I	B	O	E	S

PUZZLE 27

7	8	1	5	9	3	4	2	6
5	3	2	4	7	6	9	8	1
6	4	9	1	2	8	3	7	5
4	1	7	8	6	5	2	9	3
8	9	5	3	1	2	7	6	4
3	2	6	7	4	9	1	5	8
9	6	3	2	5	1	8	4	7
1	5	4	9	8	7	6	3	2
2	7	8	6	3	4	5	1	9

PUZZLE 28

4	7	9	8	6	3	2	1	5
5	2	6	7	9	1	4	3	8
1	8	3	2	4	5	7	9	6
2	1	8	6	3	7	9	5	4
9	5	4	1	8	2	3	6	7
3	6	7	4	5	9	1	8	2
7	4	5	9	1	6	8	2	3
8	3	1	5	2	4	6	7	9
6	9	2	3	7	8	5	4	1

PUZZLE 29

R	O	S	C	H	I	N	T	A
I	C	A	T	R	N	S	H	O
N	H	T	O	A	S	C	R	I
A	N	O	S	T	R	I	C	H
S	R	H	I	O	C	A	N	T
C	T	I	H	N	A	O	S	R
H	I	N	A	C	T	R	O	S
O	S	R	N	I	H	T	A	C
T	A	C	R	S	O	H	I	N

PUZZLE 30

T	H	E	L	O	W	I	N	G
I	L	O	E	N	G	W	H	T
N	W	G	I	H	T	L	O	E
H	I	N	W	E	O	T	G	L
W	E	T	H	G	L	O	I	N
G	O	L	N	T	I	H	E	W
L	G	I	O	W	N	E	T	H
E	N	W	T	I	H	G	L	O
O	T	H	G	L	E	N	W	I

PUZZLE 31

7	5	6	1	3	2	4	9	8
1	4	8	6	7	9	5	2	3
9	2	3	5	8	4	1	7	6
6	1	4	9	2	8	7	3	5
5	9	2	3	1	7	8	6	4
3	8	7	4	5	6	9	1	2
4	3	9	7	6	5	2	8	1
8	6	5	2	9	1	3	4	7
2	7	1	8	4	3	6	5	9

PUZZLE 32

7	9	1	2	4	6	8	3	5
8	2	6	7	5	3	4	9	1
4	3	5	9	8	1	2	6	7
6	1	4	3	2	7	9	5	8
9	8	2	5	6	4	7	1	3
5	7	3	8	1	9	6	4	2
1	5	7	4	9	8	3	2	6
2	4	8	6	3	5	1	7	9
3	6	9	1	7	2	5	8	4

PUZZLE 33

3	8	5	6	9	2	7	1	4
7	4	9	3	1	8	2	6	5
2	1	6	5	4	7	3	8	9
5	6	7	2	8	4	9	3	1
8	3	2	1	5	9	6	4	7
1	9	4	7	3	6	5	2	8
9	7	1	4	2	3	8	5	6
6	5	3	8	7	1	4	9	2
4	2	8	9	6	5	1	7	3

PUZZLE 34

9	7	8	1	2	3	5	6	4
2	4	5	9	7	6	8	1	3
6	3	1	8	4	5	9	7	2
7	2	9	6	5	1	4	3	8
1	5	4	7	3	8	2	9	6
3	8	6	4	9	2	7	5	1
5	9	2	3	6	4	1	8	7
8	6	7	2	1	9	3	4	5
4	1	3	5	8	7	6	2	9

PUZZLE 35

G	S	I	O	T	U	H	E	R
R	H	U	G	E	S	O	T	I
T	O	E	R	I	H	S	U	G
I	T	S	E	R	G	U	O	H
H	E	R	U	S	O	I	G	T
U	G	O	T	H	I	R	S	E
E	U	H	S	G	R	T	I	O
S	R	G	I	O	T	E	H	U
O	I	T	H	U	E	G	R	S

PUZZLE 36

R	F	C	L	I	E	A	M	U
M	A	L	C	F	U	I	R	E
E	I	U	M	A	R	L	F	C
C	L	F	U	E	A	R	I	M
A	M	E	R	C	I	F	U	L
U	R	I	F	M	L	C	E	A
L	C	R	I	U	M	E	A	F
F	U	A	E	R	C	M	L	I
I	E	M	A	L	F	U	C	R

PUZZLE 37

3	1	4	8	6	2	7	9	5
6	7	5	3	9	1	4	8	2
9	2	8	4	7	5	6	1	3
1	4	6	9	5	7	2	3	8
2	9	7	6	3	8	5	4	1
5	8	3	2	1	4	9	7	6
7	3	1	5	2	9	8	6	4
4	6	2	7	8	3	1	5	9
8	5	9	1	4	6	3	2	7

PUZZLE 38

5	8	2	4	7	3	6	9	1
9	7	3	2	6	1	5	4	8
6	1	4	9	5	8	3	7	2
8	2	1	3	4	5	9	6	7
7	6	5	8	2	9	4	1	3
3	4	9	7	1	6	8	2	5
4	5	7	6	3	2	1	8	9
1	9	6	5	8	7	2	3	4
2	3	8	1	9	4	7	5	6

PUZZLE 39

4	9	7	8	1	3	6	5	2
6	2	3	7	9	5	4	1	8
5	1	8	2	6	4	3	9	7
8	4	6	9	7	2	5	3	1
1	7	9	5	3	6	8	2	4
3	5	2	4	8	1	7	6	9
9	6	5	1	4	7	2	8	3
2	8	4	3	5	9	1	7	6
7	3	1	6	2	8	9	4	5

PUZZLE 40

R	A	P	I	S	C	U	O	E
U	S	E	O	A	R	P	I	C
O	C	I	P	U	E	A	S	R
I	U	C	R	E	P	S	A	O
S	E	A	C	O	U	I	R	P
P	R	O	A	I	S	E	C	U
C	O	U	S	P	A	R	E	I
E	I	S	U	R	O	C	P	A
A	P	R	E	C	I	O	U	S

PUZZLE 41

D	E	F	U	R	W	O	L	N
O	W	U	L	D	N	E	F	R
R	N	L	F	O	E	W	D	U
N	F	R	E	L	U	D	O	W
L	D	W	R	F	O	U	N	E
E	U	O	N	W	D	L	R	F
W	O	N	D	E	R	F	U	L
F	R	E	O	U	L	N	W	D
U	L	D	W	N	F	R	E	O

PUZZLE 42

5	1	7	4	8	2	3	6	9
4	3	9	1	5	6	8	7	2
2	8	6	9	7	3	1	4	5
6	5	8	3	1	4	2	9	7
3	4	1	7	2	9	5	8	6
9	7	2	5	6	8	4	3	1
7	2	3	6	4	1	9	5	8
8	6	4	2	9	5	7	1	3
1	9	5	8	3	7	6	2	4

PUZZLE 43

5	4	1	8	6	7	2	3	9
9	2	8	5	1	3	6	7	4
3	6	7	4	9	2	5	1	8
7	5	2	1	4	6	9	8	3
8	9	3	2	7	5	4	6	1
6	1	4	3	8	9	7	5	2
1	8	5	7	2	4	3	9	6
4	7	9	6	3	8	1	2	5
2	3	6	9	5	1	8	4	7

PUZZLE 44

5	3	2	1	8	6	4	9	7
9	7	4	2	3	5	6	1	8
8	6	1	9	7	4	3	5	2
2	9	5	6	4	3	8	7	1
7	1	3	5	2	8	9	6	4
4	8	6	7	9	1	5	2	3
6	5	8	3	1	7	2	4	9
3	2	7	4	6	9	1	8	5
1	4	9	8	5	2	7	3	6

PUZZLE 45

S	H	O	T	W	D	I	G	U
T	W	G	I	U	O	D	S	H
U	D	I	H	G	S	W	T	O
D	I	S	U	H	G	O	W	T
W	G	T	S	O	I	U	H	D
O	U	H	D	T	W	S	I	G
I	T	U	O	S	H	G	D	W
G	O	D	W	I	T	H	U	S
H	S	W	G	D	U	T	O	I

PUZZLE 46

B	P	L	U	N	S	C	I	A
S	C	N	I	B	A	U	P	L
I	A	U	C	P	L	B	S	N
A	L	C	P	S	N	I	U	B
N	I	S	A	U	B	P	L	C
P	U	B	L	I	C	A	N	S
C	N	P	S	A	I	L	B	U
U	S	A	B	L	P	N	C	I
L	B	I	N	C	U	S	A	P

PUZZLE 47

3	7	1	6	2	9	4	8	5
4	2	8	1	3	5	6	7	9
6	9	5	7	4	8	1	3	2
1	4	3	8	9	2	5	6	7
9	5	7	3	1	6	2	4	8
2	8	6	5	7	4	9	1	3
8	1	4	2	5	3	7	9	6
7	3	2	9	6	1	8	5	4
5	6	9	4	8	7	3	2	1

PUZZLE 48

4	9	3	6	7	2	1	5	8
2	5	1	8	9	4	7	3	6
7	8	6	3	1	5	9	2	4
3	7	8	5	4	9	2	6	1
5	1	9	2	3	6	8	4	7
6	4	2	7	8	1	5	9	3
1	3	5	9	6	7	4	8	2
8	2	7	4	5	3	6	1	9
9	6	4	1	2	8	3	7	5

PUZZLE 49

A	V	Y	I	R	D	E	S	N
R	I	D	S	N	E	Y	V	A
S	N	E	V	Y	A	R	D	I
V	E	R	Y	I	S	N	A	D
D	Y	S	N	A	R	V	I	E
I	A	N	E	D	V	S	R	Y
E	R	I	A	S	N	D	Y	V
N	D	A	R	V	Y	I	E	S
Y	S	V	D	E	I	A	N	R

PUZZLE 50

O	H	G	R	S	I	N	B	E
B	R	S	N	O	E	I	H	G
N	E	I	G	H	B	O	R	S
G	I	B	O	E	R	H	S	N
R	N	O	S	I	H	E	G	B
E	S	H	B	N	G	R	O	I
S	O	R	E	B	N	G	I	H
I	G	E	H	R	S	B	N	O
H	B	N	I	G	O	S	E	R

PUZZLE 51

9	3	6	5	2	4	8	7	1
5	2	4	1	8	7	3	9	6
8	1	7	3	9	6	5	2	4
3	8	9	7	5	1	6	4	2
6	4	1	2	3	9	7	5	8
2	7	5	4	6	8	1	3	9
4	6	2	8	7	3	9	1	5
7	5	8	9	1	2	4	6	3
1	9	3	6	4	5	2	8	7

PUZZLE 52

8	9	7	6	4	1	3	5	2
2	6	5	3	9	8	7	1	4
3	1	4	5	7	2	6	8	9
5	7	9	2	8	4	1	6	3
4	3	8	1	5	6	2	9	7
6	2	1	9	3	7	5	4	8
7	5	3	8	6	9	4	2	1
9	4	2	7	1	5	8	3	6
1	8	6	4	2	3	9	7	5

PUZZLE 53

4	9	3	8	2	6	5	1	7
2	1	5	4	7	9	6	8	3
6	8	7	1	5	3	9	2	4
3	2	9	5	8	4	1	7	6
7	6	8	9	3	1	4	5	2
5	4	1	2	6	7	8	3	9
8	5	4	3	9	2	7	6	1
9	7	2	6	1	8	3	4	5
1	3	6	7	4	5	2	9	8

PUZZLE 54

L	S	C	E	I	O	K	T	V
I	E	T	V	K	L	C	O	S
V	K	O	C	S	T	E	I	L
E	L	V	K	O	I	T	S	C
S	O	I	T	C	V	L	K	E
T	C	K	L	E	S	I	V	O
O	T	L	I	V	E	S	C	K
C	I	S	O	L	K	V	E	T
K	V	E	S	T	C	O	L	I

PUZZLE 55

H	O	N	G	R	E	T	D	A
E	A	D	T	O	N	H	G	R
T	R	G	H	A	D	E	O	N
G	T	A	E	H	R	D	N	O
N	H	O	A	D	T	R	E	G
R	D	E	O	N	G	A	T	H
A	N	H	D	T	O	G	R	E
D	G	R	N	E	A	O	H	T
O	E	T	R	G	H	N	A	D

PUZZLE 56

6	3	8	1	9	7	4	5	2
9	2	7	8	4	5	1	3	6
4	1	5	3	2	6	9	8	7
8	9	1	4	6	3	2	7	5
3	4	2	5	7	9	6	1	8
5	7	6	2	8	1	3	4	9
7	6	3	9	5	4	8	2	1
1	8	9	7	3	2	5	6	4
2	5	4	6	1	8	7	9	3

PUZZLE 57

6	1	9	5	3	4	7	2	8
3	7	8	9	1	2	6	5	4
5	2	4	7	8	6	9	1	3
7	9	1	2	4	3	8	6	5
4	6	3	1	5	8	2	9	7
8	5	2	6	9	7	3	4	1
1	4	6	8	7	9	5	3	2
2	8	5	3	6	1	4	7	9
9	3	7	4	2	5	1	8	6

PUZZLE 58

3	2	1	7	6	4	5	9	8
5	4	7	9	8	3	6	1	2
6	8	9	1	5	2	4	3	7
2	5	8	4	9	1	3	7	6
1	3	4	6	7	5	8	2	9
7	9	6	3	2	8	1	5	4
9	7	3	8	1	6	2	4	5
4	6	5	2	3	9	7	8	1
8	1	2	5	4	7	9	6	3

PUZZLE 59

H	R	A	L	G	K	I	D	T
L	I	G	H	T	D	A	R	K
T	K	D	R	A	I	H	G	L
I	A	H	T	L	R	D	K	G
G	T	R	D	K	H	L	I	A
K	D	L	A	I	G	T	H	R
A	H	K	I	R	T	G	L	D
R	L	I	G	D	A	K	T	H
D	G	T	K	H	L	R	A	I

PUZZLE 60

O	R	N	J	D	T	A	H	E
D	A	E	O	R	H	T	N	J
T	H	J	N	A	E	O	R	D
R	O	D	A	N	J	E	T	H
N	J	T	E	H	O	D	A	R
H	E	A	D	T	R	N	J	O
A	T	H	R	O	D	J	E	N
J	N	O	H	E	A	R	D	T
E	D	R	T	J	N	H	O	A

PUZZLE 61

5	3	6	2	9	4	7	8	1
2	4	1	3	7	8	6	9	5
9	7	8	1	6	5	2	3	4
4	5	2	8	3	6	9	1	7
7	8	3	5	1	9	4	2	6
6	1	9	4	2	7	3	5	8
8	9	4	6	5	3	1	7	2
1	6	7	9	8	2	5	4	3
3	2	5	7	4	1	8	6	9

PUZZLE 62

9	8	5	2	3	4	7	1	6
1	7	4	9	6	5	2	8	3
3	6	2	7	1	8	5	9	4
5	4	3	8	7	6	1	2	9
2	1	8	5	9	3	4	6	7
6	9	7	1	4	2	8	3	5
4	2	9	6	5	1	3	7	8
7	5	1	3	8	9	6	4	2
8	3	6	4	2	7	9	5	1

PUZZLE 63

2	4	3	8	6	7	5	9	1
5	6	9	3	1	4	7	8	2
7	8	1	9	5	2	3	4	6
9	2	6	4	7	8	1	3	5
8	7	4	1	3	5	2	6	9
3	1	5	6	2	9	4	7	8
6	9	7	2	4	1	8	5	3
1	5	8	7	9	3	6	2	4
4	3	2	5	8	6	9	1	7

PUZZLE 64

A	H	T	S	L	D	I	F	N
F	S	L	I	N	T	H	A	D
I	D	N	H	A	F	S	L	T
N	L	A	F	D	H	T	S	I
D	T	H	L	I	S	A	N	F
S	F	I	A	T	N	D	H	L
H	N	S	D	F	I	L	T	A
L	I	F	T	H	A	N	D	S
T	A	D	N	S	L	F	I	H

PUZZLE 65

T	U	R	F	H	N	D	E	O
D	N	O	E	T	R	U	H	F
F	E	H	U	O	D	N	R	T
E	F	D	N	U	O	R	T	H
N	H	T	R	D	F	E	O	U
R	O	U	T	E	H	F	D	N
H	R	E	O	F	U	T	N	D
U	D	N	H	R	T	O	F	E
O	T	F	D	N	E	H	U	R

PUZZLE 66

6	4	8	3	2	7	9	1	5
3	1	5	8	9	6	2	4	7
2	9	7	5	4	1	8	6	3
4	2	3	1	7	8	5	9	6
1	8	6	9	5	3	7	2	4
7	5	9	4	6	2	1	3	8
8	7	2	6	3	9	4	5	1
9	6	4	7	1	5	3	8	2
5	3	1	2	8	4	6	7	9

PUZZLE 67

3	2	5	1	6	8	7	9	4
9	1	6	2	7	4	5	3	8
8	4	7	9	5	3	2	6	1
7	9	8	4	2	6	1	5	3
2	3	1	7	8	5	9	4	6
5	6	4	3	9	1	8	2	7
6	8	2	5	3	7	4	1	9
1	5	3	8	4	9	6	7	2
4	7	9	6	1	2	3	8	5

PUZZLE 68

7	9	8	4	5	1	2	6	3
6	2	4	9	7	3	8	5	1
3	1	5	2	8	6	9	7	4
4	7	6	8	9	2	3	1	5
9	5	2	3	1	7	4	8	6
8	3	1	5	6	4	7	9	2
1	8	3	7	2	5	6	4	9
5	4	9	6	3	8	1	2	7
2	6	7	1	4	9	5	3	8

PUZZLE 69

A	P	S	H	R	C	U	D	E
R	D	H	A	E	U	P	C	S
E	C	U	S	D	P	R	H	A
C	S	E	R	U	D	A	P	H
P	U	R	C	H	A	S	E	D
H	A	D	E	P	S	C	U	R
S	R	P	D	C	H	E	A	U
D	E	C	U	A	R	H	S	P
U	H	A	P	S	E	D	R	C

PUZZLE 70

H	U	D	W	O	N	S	T	I
T	W	S	U	D	I	O	N	H
I	N	O	T	S	H	U	D	W
W	H	U	I	N	S	T	O	D
S	O	I	D	W	T	H	U	N
N	D	T	H	U	O	W	I	S
D	T	N	S	H	U	I	W	O
U	S	W	O	I	D	N	H	T
O	I	H	N	T	W	D	S	U

PUZZLE 71

3	8	9	4	7	2	6	5	1
1	2	4	3	5	6	7	8	9
7	5	6	8	9	1	3	2	4
9	4	5	2	1	7	8	6	3
2	7	3	9	6	8	1	4	5
6	1	8	5	4	3	9	7	2
5	6	1	7	3	4	2	9	8
8	9	7	1	2	5	4	3	6
4	3	2	6	8	9	5	1	7

PUZZLE 72

9	2	5	1	8	4	7	6	3
6	4	3	9	2	7	1	8	5
8	7	1	5	3	6	2	4	9
3	6	7	8	1	9	5	2	4
5	9	8	7	4	2	6	3	1
2	1	4	6	5	3	8	9	7
7	8	9	3	6	5	4	1	2
1	5	2	4	9	8	3	7	6
4	3	6	2	7	1	9	5	8

PUZZLE 73

H	S	T	N	I	O	E	F	G
G	E	I	H	F	T	N	O	S
N	O	F	S	G	E	I	T	H
O	T	H	I	E	S	F	G	N
E	F	G	T	N	H	S	I	O
S	I	N	G	O	F	T	H	E
F	H	S	O	T	N	G	E	I
T	G	O	E	S	I	H	N	F
I	N	E	F	H	G	O	S	T

PUZZLE 74

U	T	A	D	S	G	H	R	E
D	R	E	A	H	T	S	G	U
S	H	G	U	R	E	A	D	T
A	D	R	G	E	U	T	S	H
G	U	T	H	A	S	D	E	R
H	E	S	T	D	R	U	A	G
R	A	H	E	U	D	G	T	S
T	S	D	R	G	H	E	U	A
E	G	U	S	T	A	R	H	D

PUZZLE 75

1	9	4	3	5	2	7	6	8
5	7	3	6	1	8	4	2	9
6	8	2	7	4	9	3	1	5
7	6	8	5	3	4	1	9	2
4	2	1	9	8	6	5	7	3
9	3	5	1	2	7	8	4	6
2	1	9	8	7	3	6	5	4
3	4	7	2	6	5	9	8	1
8	5	6	4	9	1	2	3	7

PUZZLE 76

H	O	N	T	R	G	K	A	E
R	K	E	A	O	N	T	G	H
G	A	T	H	E	K	R	O	N
O	R	G	N	T	H	A	E	K
E	H	A	G	K	O	N	R	T
T	N	K	R	A	E	G	H	O
K	T	H	E	G	A	O	N	R
N	G	O	K	H	R	E	T	A
A	E	R	O	N	T	H	K	G

PUZZLE 77

U	I	E	O	T	R	L	N	B
O	N	B	I	L	E	T	U	R
L	T	R	N	B	U	I	O	E
B	R	I	E	O	N	U	T	L
T	O	L	U	R	B	N	E	I
E	U	N	T	I	L	R	B	O
N	B	T	L	E	I	O	R	U
R	L	U	B	N	O	E	I	T
I	E	O	R	U	T	B	L	N

PUZZLE 78

3	6	9	1	7	2	8	5	4
7	1	4	3	5	8	9	6	2
5	8	2	9	4	6	3	1	7
9	3	1	8	2	7	5	4	6
2	5	6	4	9	3	7	8	1
4	7	8	6	1	5	2	3	9
8	2	3	7	6	1	4	9	5
1	4	5	2	3	9	6	7	8
6	9	7	5	8	4	1	2	3

PUZZLE 79

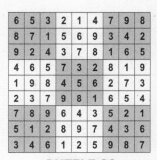

6	5	3	2	1	4	7	9	8
8	7	1	5	6	9	3	4	2
9	2	4	3	7	8	1	6	5
4	6	5	7	3	2	8	1	9
1	9	8	4	5	6	2	7	3
2	3	7	9	8	1	6	5	4
7	8	9	6	4	3	5	2	1
5	1	2	8	9	7	4	3	6
3	4	6	1	2	5	9	8	7

PUZZLE 80

3	1	9	8	7	5	4	2	6
5	6	4	9	3	2	8	7	1
7	8	2	4	1	6	9	5	3
9	5	6	1	2	8	3	4	7
4	3	7	6	5	9	1	8	2
8	2	1	7	4	3	6	9	5
6	7	5	3	8	4	2	1	9
1	9	8	2	6	7	5	3	4
2	4	3	5	9	1	7	6	8

PUZZLE 81

I	C	F	L	U	O	R	E	D
D	U	R	I	C	E	O	F	L
L	O	E	F	R	D	U	C	I
U	D	C	E	O	R	L	I	F
E	R	I	D	F	L	C	O	U
O	F	L	C	I	U	E	D	R
F	I	U	R	E	C	D	L	O
R	E	D	O	L	I	F	U	C
C	L	O	U	D	F	I	R	E

PUZZLE 82

O	E	T	D	S	N	A	K	Y
K	S	D	Y	A	O	N	T	E
Y	N	A	K	T	E	O	S	D
E	A	Y	T	D	S	K	O	N
S	T	N	E	O	K	Y	D	A
D	O	K	A	N	Y	S	E	T
A	D	S	N	K	T	E	Y	O
N	Y	O	S	E	D	T	A	K
T	K	E	O	Y	A	D	N	S

PUZZLE 83

L	O	W	E	R	T	H	A	N
R	H	T	O	A	N	W	E	L
N	E	A	L	H	W	R	O	T
T	A	N	W	O	R	E	L	H
O	L	H	T	E	A	N	R	W
E	W	R	H	N	L	O	T	A
H	R	L	A	W	O	T	N	E
A	N	E	R	T	H	L	W	O
W	T	O	N	L	E	A	H	R

PUZZLE 84

I	R	M	N	S	E	O	B	T
E	B	O	M	I	T	S	R	N
N	T	S	R	O	B	M	I	E
T	E	N	I	B	S	R	M	O
M	O	B	T	N	R	E	S	I
R	S	I	O	E	M	N	T	B
S	N	T	E	R	I	B	O	M
B	M	E	S	T	O	I	N	R
O	I	R	B	M	N	T	E	S

PUZZLE 85

O	W	E	A	K	B	R	N	S
N	R	K	E	S	W	O	A	B
B	S	A	N	O	R	W	K	E
A	B	N	O	W	S	E	R	K
E	K	W	R	B	A	N	S	O
S	O	R	K	E	N	A	B	W
W	A	S	B	R	O	K	E	N
R	E	O	S	N	K	B	W	A
K	N	B	W	A	E	S	O	R

PUZZLE 86

I	N	R	O	S	E	H	P	T
T	H	E	P	R	I	S	O	N
S	O	P	T	N	H	R	E	I
H	R	I	E	P	S	N	T	O
N	E	T	I	H	O	P	S	R
O	P	S	R	T	N	I	H	E
R	T	H	N	E	P	O	I	S
P	I	N	S	O	T	E	R	H
E	S	O	H	I	R	T	N	P

PUZZLE 87

1	8	5	9	3	2	6	4	7
9	2	4	8	6	7	3	1	5
7	3	6	4	5	1	2	8	9
8	9	2	3	7	4	1	5	6
5	6	3	1	8	9	7	2	4
4	7	1	5	2	6	8	9	3
2	5	8	6	9	3	4	7	1
6	4	9	7	1	8	5	3	2
3	1	7	2	4	5	9	6	8

PUZZLE 88

1	9	3	7	5	8	6	2	4
2	8	7	4	3	6	9	1	5
4	6	5	1	2	9	7	3	8
9	1	2	5	7	3	4	8	6
5	7	8	2	6	4	3	9	1
3	4	6	9	8	1	2	5	7
6	5	1	3	4	2	8	7	9
8	2	9	6	1	7	5	4	3
7	3	4	8	9	5	1	6	2

PUZZLE 89

2	1	5	6	8	3	7	9	4
4	7	8	1	2	9	6	5	3
3	6	9	7	4	5	8	2	1
8	4	7	9	1	2	3	6	5
5	3	2	8	7	6	4	1	9
6	9	1	5	3	4	2	8	7
9	8	3	2	5	7	1	4	6
1	5	4	3	6	8	9	7	2
7	2	6	4	9	1	5	3	8

PUZZLE 90

H	I	V	F	W	O	T	A	R
O	T	W	A	R	H	I	F	V
F	R	A	V	I	T	W	H	O
R	W	T	O	H	I	A	V	F
V	O	F	R	T	A	H	W	I
I	A	H	W	F	V	O	R	T
T	H	R	I	V	W	F	O	A
W	V	O	T	A	F	R	I	H
A	F	I	H	O	R	V	T	W

PUZZLE 91

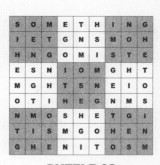

S	O	M	E	T	H	I	N	G
I	E	T	G	N	S	M	O	H
H	N	G	O	M	I	S	T	E
E	S	N	I	O	M	G	H	T
M	G	H	T	S	N	E	I	O
O	T	I	H	E	G	N	M	S
N	M	O	S	H	E	T	G	I
T	I	S	M	G	O	H	E	N
G	H	E	N	I	T	O	S	M

PUZZLE 92

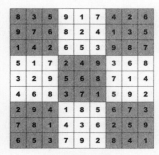

4	8	5	6	9	3	2	1	7
7	1	6	8	5	2	4	3	9
3	9	2	4	7	1	6	8	5
1	5	7	2	8	4	3	9	6
2	6	4	3	1	9	5	7	8
8	3	9	7	6	5	1	4	2
6	4	1	9	2	8	7	5	3
5	2	8	1	3	7	9	6	4
9	7	3	5	4	6	8	2	1

PUZZLE 93

9	5	3	6	2	7	1	8	4
6	7	4	1	8	9	5	3	2
8	2	1	3	5	4	7	6	9
4	3	2	8	6	5	9	7	1
5	8	7	9	4	1	3	2	6
1	9	6	7	3	2	8	4	5
3	1	8	2	9	6	4	5	7
2	4	9	5	7	3	6	1	8
7	6	5	4	1	8	2	9	3

PUZZLE 94

8	3	5	9	1	7	4	2	6
9	7	6	8	2	4	1	3	5
1	4	2	6	5	3	9	8	7
5	1	7	2	4	9	3	6	8
3	2	9	5	6	8	7	1	4
4	6	8	3	7	1	5	9	2
2	9	4	1	8	5	6	7	3
7	8	1	4	3	6	2	5	9
6	5	3	7	9	2	8	4	1

PUZZLE 95

L	H	F	M	I	S	E	T	O
E	I	T	O	H	L	F	M	S
O	M	S	E	F	T	I	H	L
I	S	O	H	L	M	T	E	F
F	E	M	S	T	O	L	I	H
T	L	H	I	E	F	S	O	M
H	F	L	T	O	E	M	S	I
M	T	I	F	S	H	O	L	E
S	O	E	L	M	I	H	F	T

PUZZLE 96

O	C	U	E	N	R	L	S	I
E	S	N	I	L	C	U	O	R
L	R	I	U	S	O	E	C	N
C	O	R	N	E	L	I	U	S
S	I	L	O	C	U	N	R	E
N	U	E	R	I	S	O	L	C
R	N	C	L	O	I	S	E	U
U	E	O	S	R	N	C	I	L
I	L	S	C	U	E	R	N	O

PUZZLE 97

3	2	9	5	8	7	1	6	4
8	6	4	9	3	1	7	2	5
1	5	7	6	2	4	3	9	8
9	3	6	7	4	8	2	5	1
4	7	1	3	5	2	6	8	9
5	8	2	1	6	9	4	7	3
2	1	3	8	9	6	5	4	7
7	4	8	2	1	5	9	3	6
6	9	5	4	7	3	8	1	2

PUZZLE 98

7	2	4	6	3	5	8	9	1
3	8	1	7	2	9	5	4	6
6	5	9	4	8	1	3	2	7
8	4	7	1	9	6	2	5	3
5	6	3	8	4	2	1	7	9
9	1	2	5	7	3	6	8	4
1	7	8	2	6	4	9	3	5
2	9	6	3	5	7	4	1	8
4	3	5	9	1	8	7	6	2

PUZZLE 99

8	2	6	1	5	7	9	4	3
7	3	9	2	4	8	6	1	5
4	1	5	9	6	3	2	7	8
5	7	2	8	9	6	1	3	4
6	8	3	4	1	5	7	2	9
9	4	1	7	3	2	5	8	6
2	6	7	5	8	4	3	9	1
3	9	8	6	7	1	4	5	2
1	5	4	3	2	9	8	6	7

PUZZLE 100

4	6	5	7	1	3	9	8	2
1	8	3	2	9	4	5	7	6
7	9	2	8	6	5	1	3	4
2	4	1	6	7	8	3	9	5
5	7	9	4	3	1	6	2	8
8	3	6	9	5	2	7	4	1
6	1	4	3	8	7	2	5	9
9	2	7	5	4	6	8	1	3
3	5	8	1	2	9	4	6	7

PUZZLE 101

Z	I	N	M	B	E	H	O	R
M	O	B	H	N	R	I	E	Z
E	R	H	O	I	Z	M	B	N
H	M	O	E	R	N	B	Z	I
N	E	I	B	Z	O	R	M	H
B	Z	R	I	M	H	O	N	E
O	H	Z	R	E	M	N	I	B
R	B	E	N	O	I	Z	H	M
I	N	M	Z	H	B	E	R	O

PUZZLE 102

O	L	K	I	G	N	S	H	D
I	H	G	D	O	S	K	L	N
N	D	S	H	L	K	G	O	I
L	S	I	O	N	G	D	K	H
H	N	O	K	D	L	I	S	G
G	K	D	S	I	H	O	N	L
D	O	L	N	S	I	H	G	K
K	I	N	G	H	O	L	D	S
S	G	H	L	K	D	N	I	O

PUZZLE 103

8	5	2	3	4	7	6	9	1
4	1	7	9	8	6	2	5	3
3	6	9	5	1	2	7	8	4
1	4	5	8	7	9	3	6	2
9	7	3	6	2	5	1	4	8
2	8	6	1	3	4	5	7	9
6	3	4	2	5	8	9	1	7
7	9	1	4	6	3	8	2	5
5	2	8	7	9	1	4	3	6

PUZZLE 104